HOME ACCENTS IN A FLASH

Timesaving Projects & Ideas

The Home Decorating Institute®

Copyright © 1996 Cowles Creative Publishing, Inc., formerly Cy DeCosse Incorporated
5900 Green Oak Drive Minnetonka, Minnesota 55343 • 1-800-328-3895 • All rights reserved • Printed in U.S.A.

Library of Congress Cataloging-in-Publication Data Home accents in a flash / the Home Decorating Institute. p. cm. — (Arts & crafts for home decorating) Includes index. ISBN 0-86573-387-2 (hardcover) — ISBN 0-86573-388-0 (softcover) 1. House furnishings. 2. Handicraft. 3. Interior decoration. I. Home Decorating Institute (Minnetonka, Minn.) II. Cy DeCosse Incorporated. III. Series. TT387.H66 1996 747 — dc20 96-1753

CONTENTS

Decorating with Fabric

Simple Slipcovers 8

Furniture Face-lifts with Linens . . . 14

Draped Window Treatments 20

Triangular Bed Canopies 26

Instant Bed Skirts 31

Easy Bolster Pillows 32

Flanged & Fringed Pillows 35

Decorating the Walls

Texturizing Techniques
with Paint 42

Color Washing Walls 46

Freehand Painted Designs
for Walls 48

Creative Wall Borders 52

Ribbon-framed Walls 59

Floral Accents

Easy Grapevine Wreaths 67

Quick Containers for
  Fresh Flowers 72

Single-variety Arrangements 77

Dried Floral Arrangements 82

Quick Floral Displays 84

Creative Accessories

Spray Painting Techniques 92

Special Effects with Spray Paint . . . 95

Copper Foil Picture Frames 98

Rustic Frames 102

Rub-on Transfers 107

Switch Plate Cover-ups 108

Customized Lamp Shades 115

Terra-cotta Accessories 120

Shelf Edgings 124

HOME ACCENTS IN A FLASH

Decorating your home with style and interest doesn't have to consume all of your free time.

Busy lifestyles with limited leisure time often cause frustration when it comes to home decorating. In spite of the satisfaction derived from doing it yourself, the time commitment involved can deter even the most avid home decorating enthusiast.

There are, however, decorating shortcuts and timesaving tips that can help you maximize your efforts. Careful planning and organizing of materials shorten the time needed to complete any project. There are also many tools and products on the market designed to save time.

Above all, imagination and an acceptance of the imperfect are necessary to make shortcut decorating successful. Open your mind to the possibility of using ordinary objects to achieve impressive results. Use decorative chain or corrugated cardboard to create an interesting border around a room. Texturize a wall, applying a glaze with crumpled paper or coarse fabric. Or update a room with easy slipcovers made from bed linens.

Relax your expectations and allow imperfections to give character to your decorating scheme. Decorate a wall with freehand painted designs or make rustic picture frames from weathered wood, accepting slight imperfections as an integral part of the finished project.

Create instant decorating impact with easy floral accents and eye-catching accessories. Make beautiful, draping window treatments or bed canopies in minutes with little or no sewing. Timesaving techniques and ideas help you create the look you want while giving you more time to sit back and enjoy it.

Decorating
with Fabric

SIMPLE SLIPCOVERS

Upholstered furniture can be given a quick makeover with casual, unstructured slipcovers. An armchair can be transformed in minutes, by draping it with a bed sheet or several yards of fabric. Loose shaping is achieved by tucking excess fabric into the crevices of the chair and securing fullness at the corners. The ends of the sheet may be tied into a large knot at the back of the chair. Or a decorative cord can be tied around the chair to hold the fabric slipcover in place.

An armless chair can be draped gracefully with a length of decorator fabric and tied with a ribbon or cord at the back of the seat. Hems can be sewn, if desired, or neat, narrow selvages can be left exposed.

Decorator fabric (right), cut into two lengths, is draped sideways over the seat and back of an armchair. Excess fabric is tucked around the cushion and folded out at the chair back. Decorative cord adds a finishing touch.

King-size sheet (opposite) becomes an instant slipcover for an armchair. Excess fabric is tied out at the front corners and into a large, loose knot at the chair back.

Armless side chairs (lower right) are draped from front to back with decorator fabric. Brocade ribbons, secured at the backs of the seats, hold the slipcovers in place.

HOW TO SLIPCOVER AN ARMCHAIR WITH A SHEET

MATERIALS

- One flat king-size bed sheet.
- Cord or narrow grosgrain ribbon, for tying excess fullness at corners.
- Polyurethane foam, 2" (5 cm) thick, cut into three strips, 2" (5 cm) wide, with lengths equal to sides and back of seat cushion.

1 Drape sheet over chair, with decorative sheet hem just above floor at front of chair and excess fabric width distributed evenly at sides.

2 Tuck excess sheet fabric into crevices around seat cushion, until sheet reaches desired length at sides; smooth sheet over arms toward chair back. Insert foam strips into crevices to help hold sheet in place.

3 Tie excess sheet fabric at back of chair into large knot, keeping grain of the sheet hanging parallel to floor at sides of chair.

4 Tie out excess fullness at front corners on underside of slipcover, using cord or ribbon.

HOW TO SLIPCOVER AN ARMCHAIR WITH FABRIC

MATERIALS

- 6 to 7 yd. (5.5 to 6.4 m) fabric, 54" to 60" (137 to 152.5 cm) wide, depending on size of chair; select fabric with solid color or nondirectional print.

- Polyurethane foam, 2" (5 cm) thick, cut into three strips, 2" (5 cm) wide, with lengths equal to sides and back of seat cushion.

- Twist pins, optional.

- Decorative cord, with length equal to circumference of chair plus additional length for tying knot.

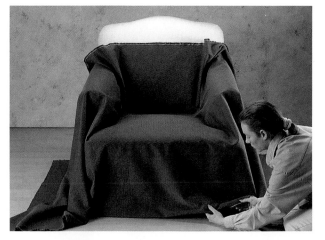

1 Cut the fabric into two equal lengths. Drape one length of fabric horizontally over seat and arms of the chair; turn under selvage, and puddle the fabric slightly on floor at front of chair, with excess fabric length distributed evenly at sides.

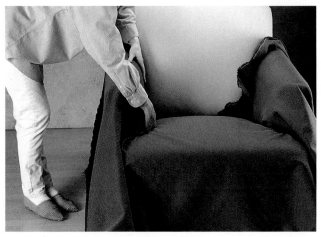

2 Tuck excess fabric into the crevices at sides and back of seat cushion, until desired amount of fabric puddles on floor at the sides; smooth fabric over the arms toward chair back.

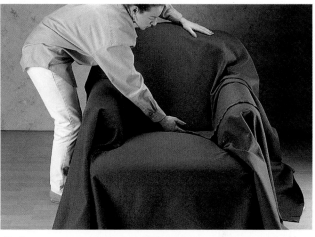

3 Drape second length of fabric horizontally over back of the chair, tucking 6" to 10" (15 to 25.5 cm) into the crevice at back of seat cushion; allow fabric to fall straight down at the sides, overlapping front of the slipcover and puddling on the floor.

4 Fold out the excess fabric diagonally at back of the chair, overlapping folds and allowing the excess length to puddle on the floor. Secure to the chair back, using twist pins, if desired.

5 Insert foam strips into crevices around cushion to help hold the fabric in place. Tie decorative cord tightly around chair, parallel to floor, just below cushion. Arrange excess fullness into gathered clusters under cord at corners of chair.

HOW TO SLIPCOVER AN ARMLESS CHAIR

MATERIALS

- Fabric, 45" to 60" (115 to 152.5 cm) wide, depending on size of chair.
- Ribbon or decorative cord.

CUTTING DIRECTIONS

Cut the fabric with the length equal to the continuous distance from the floor up the front of the chair, over the seat to the back, and up and over the back to the floor plus 2" (5 cm) for hems.

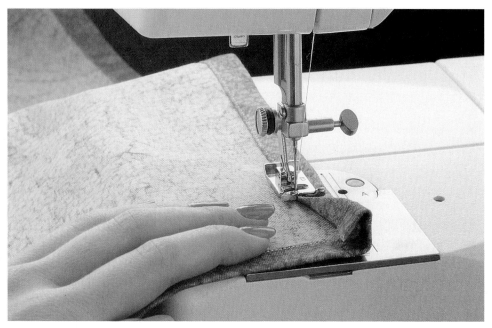

1 Press cut end under ½" (1.3 cm) twice; stitch to make double-fold hem. Repeat for opposite end. Trim selvages and hem long sides, if necessary.

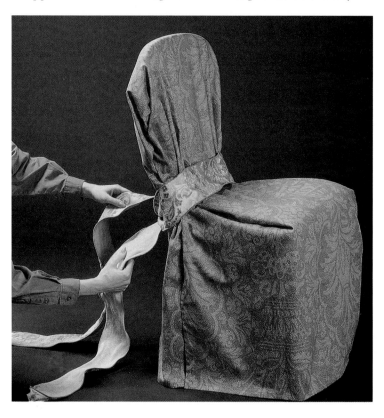

2 Drape fabric over the chair, smoothing the fabric to the back of the seat, with hemmed ends at the floor. Tuck in excess fullness at the back of chair. Wrap ribbon or cord around chair and fabric at back of the seat; knot securely at the chair back.

MORE IDEAS FOR SIMPLE SLIPCOVERS

Shimmery organza (right) is used to slipcover an ornate metal side chair, creating an alluring translucent look. Excess fabric is knotted gracefully at the back.

Sofa slipcover (below) is made from two flat queen-size sheets sewn together in the center. Make the slipcover following steps 2 and 4 on page 10, knotting excess at all corners as in step 3.

FURNITURE
FACE-LIFTS
WITH LINENS

Linens of various kinds can be used for instant furniture face-lifts. Items such as table runners, pillowcases, and kitchen towels may be used as simple slipcovers or chair drapes. Little or no sewing is required, since the linens have finished edges and are available in a wide variety of sizes.

Table runner *is used as a chair drape, giving a plain chair a fresh look. Simply remove the seat cushion, drape the runner over the chair from front to back, and replace the cushion.*

Kitchen towel *(far right) is tied at the front corners and back posts for an instant chair seat cover.*

Pillowcases *(right) are quickly transformed into a slipcover for a bedroom chair.*

HOW TO MAKE A PILLOWCASE SLIPCOVER
FOR AN ACCENT CHAIR

MATERIALS

- Upholstery batting.
- Needle and thread.
- Two standard pillowcases.
- Grosgrain ribbon.
- Safety pins.

CUTTING DIRECTIONS

Determine the desired length for the slipcover on the chair back. Cut a piece of upholstery batting 1" (2.5 cm) wider than the chair back, with the length equal to twice the desired slipcover length minus twice the depth of the pillowcase trim. Cut another piece of batting with the width and length equal to the width and length of the chair seat.

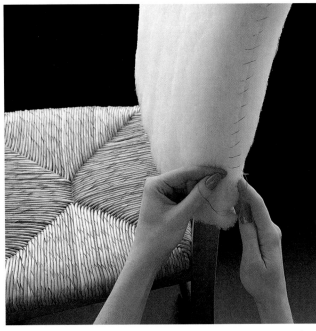

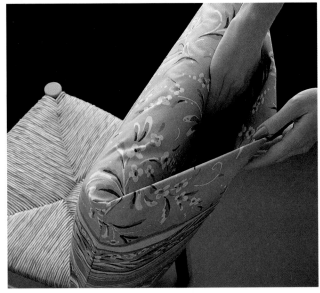

1 Wrap the batting over chair back, extending to equal lengths on front and back. Whipstitch front and back together at sides.

2 Slide the pillowcase over chair back to desired length; tuck excess pillowcase in smoothly at back of chair.

3 Determine desired drop length at chair front. Insert seat batting into second pillowcase, with front edge of batting just behind drop length.

4 Tuck excess pillowcase in smoothly under batting at back of seat slipcover.

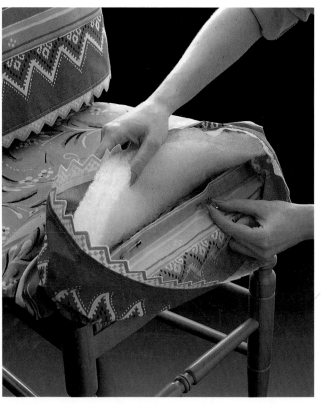

5 Tie the back corners of the seat slipcover to the chair, using lengths of grosgrain ribbon; catch batting in the tied corners.

6 Pin out excess length on underside of seat slipcover, using safety pins, allowing pillowcase trim edges to hang evenly at front of chair.

HOW TO MAKE A KITCHEN TOWEL SEAT COVER

MATERIALS

• Kitchen towel, measuring about 20" × 30" (51 × 76 cm).   • Ribbon or decorative cord.

1 Place towel sideways over chair seat. Mark positions of back posts.

2 Turn under hemmed edge ½" (1.3 cm) at marks; sew 2" (5 cm) casings, centered at the marks, back-stitching to secure. Insert ribbon or cord into casings, and tie to chair posts. Tie front corners of towel to chair legs, using ribbon or cord.

MORE IDEAS FOR DECORATING WITH LINENS

Table topper *is used for an ottoman slip-cover. The corners of the table topper are tied to the ottoman legs, using decorative cord. Large tassels add an elegant touch.*

Battenberg lace table runner *is used as a valance for a shower curtain. Attach the runner to the rod along with the curtain, or attach it to a separate rod for a stationary valance.*

Casual dinner napkins, *overlapped and draped diagonally, make a charming mantel cloth for a country home.*

DRAPED WINDOW TREATMENTS

Soft, draping window treatments can be made quickly, using sheer to lightweight reversible fabrics. Since the treatments are made without side hems or seams, it is important to use fabric with neat, narrow selvages. Lace fabrics with finished side edges are also suitable. Though lace is technically not reversible, it usually takes close inspection to distinguish right from wrong sides.

Suitable fabrics may vary in width from 48" to 60" (122 to 152.5 cm). The number of fabric widths needed depends on the width of the window and the style of the treatment. Experiment with inexpensive fabric to determine the number of fabric widths needed.

Several options are available for mounting the window treatment. Hanging the fabric over a decorative rod or pole mounted just above the window frame is the easiest installation method. For a unique look, the fabric can be tied to decorative hooks or knobs mounted on or above the window frame. If the treatment requires tieback holders, simple hidden tenter hooks may be used. A wide selection of decorative holders is also available.

When the treatment is mounted on a pole, the lower edge of

Lace fabric is hung over a decor-ative rod and secured at the sides of the window with holdbacks.

any flat panel will be straight and can therefore fall just below the window frame or sill, or just above the floor, if desired. A treatment tied to knobs or hooks at the top of the window frame will not have a straight lower edge. Plan to have the lower edge of this window treatment style puddle on the floor or hang unevenly 3" to 5" (7.5 to 12.5 cm) below the window frame.

MATERIALS

- Sheer to lightweight, softly draping reversible fabric with neat, narrow selvages or lace with finished edges, 48" to 60" (122 to 152.5 cm) wide; length as determined in cutting directions on pages 22 and 23.

- Decorative rod or pole and mounting brackets; or decorative hooks or knobs for mounting window treatment. Plan three hooks or knobs for first fabric width plus two hooks or knobs for each additional fabric width.

- Tenter hooks or decorative tieback holders.

- Ribbon or cord for tying fabric to knobs or hooks at top of window, or to tieback holders or tenter hooks at sides.

Reversible semisheer fabric is tied to decorative hooks above the window. The front panel is tied in a graceful knot, while the back panel puddles on the floor.

HOW TO INSTALL A DRAPED WINDOW TREATMENT ON HOOKS OR KNOBS

CUTTING DIRECTIONS

Cut each width of fabric with the length equal to twice the desired finished length of the treatment plus 40" (102 cm) for floor puddles and hems. For treatments with free-hanging uneven lower edges, cut each width of fabric with the length equal to twice the desired finished length plus 2" (5 cm) for hems.

Decorative knobs that have screws with a wood thread at one end are suitable for inserting into woodwork. Knobs that have screws without a wood thread **(a)** can be made suitable for inserting into woodwork by replacing the screw with a hanger bolt **(b).** Hanger bolts have a metal thread at one end for inserting into the knob and a wood thread at the opposite end for inserting into the woodwork. Use appropriate anchors if installing hanger bolts into drywall.

1 Install decorative hooks or knobs on or just above the window frame; position one at each outer edge, with remaining hooks or knobs evenly spaced. Tie a decorative cord or ribbon to each hook or knob, leaving long tails.

2 Hem the cut edges of fabric as in step 1 on page 23. Fold fabric in half, forming two panels, with lower edges even and hem allowances facing the window. Grasp outer edge at fold; tie to hook or knob, 2" to 3" (5 to 7.5 cm) from fold. Repeat at opposite side and again in the center. Repeat for any additional panels. Complete window treatment, using any of the styles on pages 23 through 25.

HOW TO INSTALL A DRAPED WINDOW TREATMENT ON A ROD OR POLE

CUTTING DIRECTIONS

Mount the rod or pole just above the window frame. Cut each width of fabric with the length equal to twice the desired finished length of the treatment plus 40" (102 cm) for floor puddles and hems. For pole-mounted treatments with free-hanging straight lower edges, hang a length of twill tape over the pole to the desired length, with the lower edges even. Cut the fabric 2" (5 cm) longer than the twill tape.

1 Press cut edge under ½" (1.3 cm) twice; stitch to make double-fold hem. Repeat for opposite cut end, pressing fabric in opposite direction.

2 Hang fabric over rod, forming two panels, with lower edges even and hem allowances facing the window. Complete window treatment, using any of the styles below or on pages 24 and 25.

DRAPED WINDOW TREATMENT STYLES

1 **Tiebacks.** Install tieback holders or tenter hooks at the desired height, even with outer edge of window treatment. Grasp outer edge of front fabric panel even with holder.

(Continued)

2 Gather up fabric to opposite edge, at a 45° angle toward the floor. Secure gathered panel to holder. Repeat for the opposite side of back panel, if desired.

1 **Tent flap sides.** Grasp the outer edge of front fabric panel; pull to opposite side, adjusting position of pulled-back edge as desired. Mark wall for placement of tieback holder or tenter hook; mark fabric edge with pin.

2 Install the tieback holder or tenter hook; tie the fabric edge to the holder, using ribbon or cord. Pull back and secure opposite edge of back panel, if desired.

1 Center knot. Grasp outer edges of front fabric panel about 18" (46 cm) below desired knot position. Gather up fabric on each side toward the center, gathering upward toward desired knot position.

2 Tie knot in gathered front panel; adjust sides of panel above knot as desired.

1 Side knots. Install tenter hooks at desired knot height, even with outer edge of window treatment. Grasp the outer edge of front fabric panel even with holder.

2 Gather up fabric to opposite edge, gathering at a 45° angle toward floor. Tie knot in panel; secure knot to tenter hook. Make a side knot for opposite side of back panel, if desired.

TRIANGULAR BED CANOPIES

Bed canopies are an exotic revival of the past, when fabric enveloped the bed for privacy or protection. Though purely decorative today, modern versions of the bed canopy create an aura of seclusion and draw all attention in the room to the bed.

The triangular bed canopy is a long sweep of fabric mounted high above the head of the bed, draping to points on both sides and falling to the floor. One version of the triangular bed canopy is mounted on three short rods, available in a kit, that project 15" to 22" (38 to 56 cm) straight out from the wall. Or swag holders can be used for a triangular bed canopy that is mounted closer to the wall. For a luxurious look, the fabric can be arranged in rosettes at the swag holders and allowed to puddle on the floor.

Use one full width of fabric, measuring 48" to 54" (122 to 137 cm) wide, for the triangular bed canopy. To save time, allow the selvages to remain instead of sewing side hems. Select lightweight fabric, such as lace, gauze, or netting. If other decorator fabric is preferred, side hems are only necessary when the canopy is installed on canopy rods. Otherwise, the selvages can be tucked under and hidden when the canopy is installed.

Rosettes and floor puddles (above) add a luxurious look to a simple bed canopy.

Lace canopy (opposite) is mounted on specialty rods that project straight out from the wall.

HOW TO MAKE A TRIANGULAR BED CANOPY
(MOUNTED ON RODS)

MATERIALS

- Bed canopy hardware kit, including three rods and installation brackets.
- Twill tape.
- Lightweight to sheer fabric, such as lace, gauze, or netting; or lightweight decorator fabric, if preferred.

CUTTING DIRECTIONS

Measure the circumference of the rod; add ½" (1.3 cm) ease and divide by two to determine the rod-pocket depth. Cut the fabric twice the length of the twill tape, as determined in step 1, below, plus six times the rod-pocket depth plus 4" (10 cm) for the heading on the top rod plus 8" (20.5 cm) for the bottom hems.

1 Mount rods on wall at head of bed, following manufacturer's instructions. Center one rod 84" (213.5 cm) from the floor; mount each of the other rods 45" (115 cm) from the floor, or higher to clear headboard, and 4" (10 cm) out from the sides of the bed. Drape a length of twill tape from bottom of top rod down over one side rod and stopping ½" (1.3 cm) from the floor, allowing tape to fall in gentle swoop between rods as desired for the finished canopy.

2 Cut fabric. At one end, press under 2" (5 cm) twice to wrong side; stitch to make double-fold hem, using straight stitch. Repeat for opposite end. If using decorator fabric, cut off selvages and sew 1" (2.5 cm) double-fold hems on long sides.

3 Fold fabric in half crosswise, wrong sides together; press. Mark a line 2" (5 cm) from fold for heading; mark a second line the depth of the rod pocket from the first line. Pin layers together along lines; stitch.

4 Measure up from end 45" (115 cm), or height of side rod placement plus rod-pocket depth; mark. Fold the fabric crosswise, right sides together, at mark; press. Stitch at depth of the rod pocket from the fold, using tape on bed of machine as stitching guide. Repeat for opposite end.

5 Remove rods from brackets; insert rods into rod pockets. Mount canopy. Adjust rods to desired length; distribute gathers evenly on rods.

HOW TO MAKE A TRIANGULAR BED CANOPY WITH ROSETTES & FLOOR PUDDLES (MOUNTED ON SWAG HOLDERS)

MATERIALS

- Three swag holders.
- Twill tape.
- Lightweight to sheer fabric, such as lace, gauze, or netting; or lightweight decorator fabric, if preferred.
- Strong cord or ribbon.

CUTTING DIRECTIONS

Cut the fabric twice the length of the twill tape, as determined in step 1, below, plus 100" (254.5 cm). This allows 20" (51 cm) for each rosette and floor puddle.

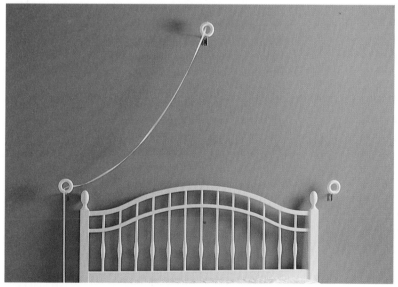

1 Mount the swag holders, following the manufacturer's instructions, in locations as described in step 1, opposite. Drape a length of twill tape from center of top holder down over one side holder to the floor, allowing the tape to fall in gentle swoop between holders as desired for finished canopy.

2 Cut fabric for canopy. Fanfold loosely across the width of the canopy, 10" (25.5 cm) to one side of center. Tie folds in place, using cord or ribbon.

(Continued)

3 Measure a distance from end equal to height of side swag holder from floor plus 40" (102 cm); fanfold loosely, and tie. Repeat for opposite end. Drape canopy over holders at points of fanfolds. Loosen ties and use to secure canopy to the holders.

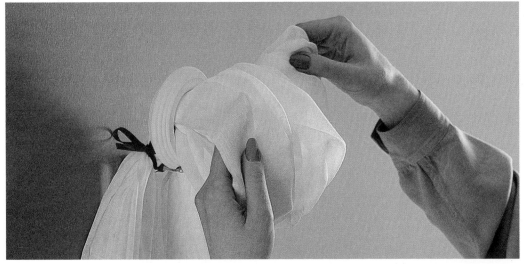

4 Fanfold the canopy loosely 20" (51 cm) below top swag holder, on the side with longer drape. Bring folded fabric up through the swag holder; tie. Spread the fabric out into rosette as desired. Repeat for side rosettes.

5 Gather the lower end into hand; tie with cord or ribbon. Tuck the tied end under, and arrange the folds of the floor puddle as desired. Repeat for opposite side.

INSTANT BED SKIRTS

Bed skirts, used in combination with duvets, comforters, and coverlets, hide the box spring and legs of the bed for an attractive, finished look. A lace bed skirt can be made quickly by securing lace valance fabric to the box spring, using elastic. Or, to coordinate with the bedding, a matching flat sheet in the same size as the bed can be slid between the box spring and mattress, making an instant bed skirt.

Lace bed skirt (above) is created by running elastic, 1" (2.5 cm) wide, through the beading holes or casing at the top of valance lace. Purchase enough lace to cover the sides and foot of the bed, adding extra fullness, if desired. Pull elastic taut around the box spring, and knot securely at the head of the bed.

A flat sheet (below), slid between the mattress and box spring, becomes an instant bed skirt. The extra width and length of the sheet that has been allowed for tuck-under at the sides and foot of the bed is just the right amount to become the drop for the bed skirt.

EASY BOLSTER PILLOWS

Create plump bolster pillows in a matter of minutes, without sewing a single stitch. Simply wrap, roll, and tie to make these unique accent pillows for the bed or sofa. For a tailored, clean look, make jelly roll bolsters. Just as the name implies, the ends of this pillow style look like a jelly roll. Or roll up romantic bolsters with rich rosettes tied at each end.

MATERIALS

- Decorator fabric, 54" (137 cm) wide; for jelly roll bolster, 1 yd. (0.95 m) if fabric is solid color or nondirectional print, or 1½ yd. (1.4 m) if fabric has directional print; for rosette bolster, 1½ yd. (1.4 m).

- Upholstery batting, 18" × 44" (46 × 112 cm).
- Strong string.
- 2 yd. (1.85 m) decorative cord or ribbon, cut in half.

HOW TO MAKE A JELLY ROLL BOLSTER

CUTTING DIRECTIONS

Cut the fabric to a width of 36" (91.5 cm), if it has a directional print.

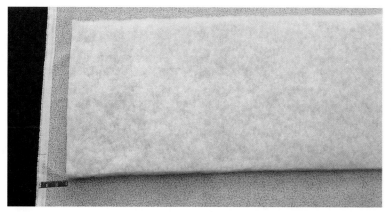

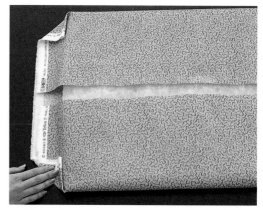

1 Place fabric facedown on work surface. Place upholstery batting over fabric, centering the width of the batting over the width of the fabric, with one short end of batting 3" (7.5 cm) from end of fabric.

2 Wrap the long edges of fabric in over the batting. Miter the fabric ends; wrap ends in over batting.

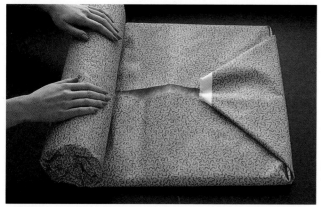

3 Roll wrapped batting, beginning at end with shorter mitered wrap. Keep fabric snug to batting, and roll with a firmness that does not crush the loft of the batting.

4 Tie string snugly around bolster about 3" (7.5 cm) from each end. Wrap cord or ribbon around bolster over the string; tie knot or bow as desired, positioning bow or knot on side opposite the end of the roll.

HOW TO MAKE A ROSETTE BOLSTER

1 Follow steps 1 and 2 above, wrapping fabric over the batting so edges meet at center of the batting, with equal extensions of folded fabric at each side. Follow step 3, above.

2 Tie the string tightly at ends of the bolster, just beyond the batting. Tie cord or ribbon over the string as desired. Arrange rosettes at ends of bolster.

FLANGED & FRINGED PILLOWS

Flanged or fringed decorator pillows can be put together in a snap. Soft, supple leathers and suedes can be made into rich flanged or fringed pillows for a living room or den. Synthetic leathers and suedes may be used as well. Or for less expense, a more casual look can be achieved by making cozy fringed pillows from reversible polyester fleece fabric.

To make the flanged pillows, leather lacing is threaded through holes that have been punched in the leather, securing the pillow front to the back. For a finishing touch, decorative buttons or conchos are tied to the corners. The tools and materials needed can be purchased at leather craft and supply stores.

Because leather, suede, and fleece do not ravel, fringed pillows are made simply by sewing and cutting. The look can be varied by lengthening or shortening the fringe, or by tying a row of knots in the fringe at the stitching line.

Fringed fleece pillow *is a cozy accent in a casual room.*

Suede pillow with knotted fringe *(opposite) is paired with a leather flanged pillow for a luxurious look.*

HOW TO MAKE A FLANGED PILLOW

MATERIALS

- Pillow form in desired size.
- Soft leather or suede, or synthetic leather or suede.
- Leather lacing.
- Leather lacing needle; needlenose pliers.
- Hole punch tool, in size appropriate for lacing; wooden or rubber mallet; cutting mat.
- Four conchos or decorative buttons.

CUTTING DIRECTIONS

Determine the desired depth of the flange, from 2" to 3½" (5 to 9 cm), depending on the size of the pillow. Cut pillow front and pillow back with sides equal to the measurements of the pillow form plus twice the desired depth of the flange.

Cut four leather lacing strips with lengths equal to the length of one side of the pillow form plus 10" (25.5 cm).

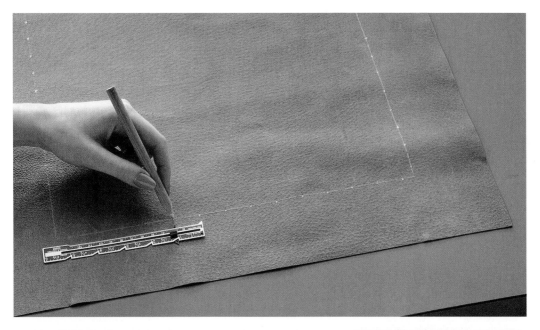

1 Mark depth of the flange with faint pencil line on wrong side of the pillow front. Mark dots for the holes along pencil line, spacing the marks 1" (2.5 cm) apart and beginning and ending ½" (1.3 cm) from each corner. There should be an even number of marks on each side.

2 Place pillow front over the pillow back, aligning edges, right sides together on cutting mat. Punch holes at the marks, using punching tool and mallet.

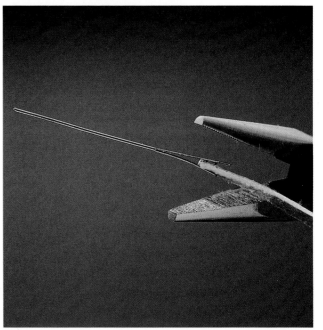

3 Open leather needle at spring end; insert lacing, with top side of lacing against prongs. Using needlenose pliers, squeeze needle so prongs pierce lacing.

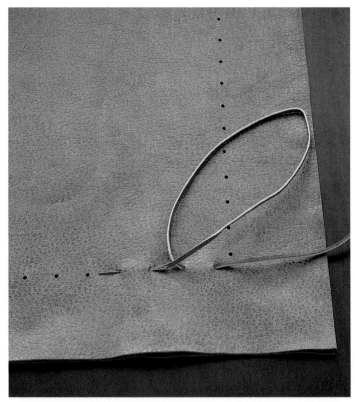

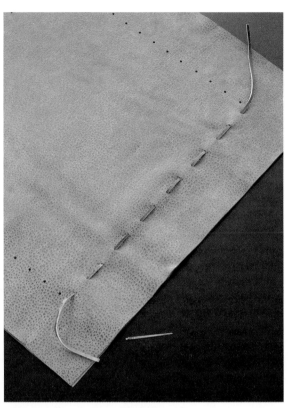

4 Place pillow front over pillow back, wrong sides together, aligning edges and holes. Beginning at one corner, insert the lacing through aligned holes from front to back; bring lacing up through next set of holes.

5 Continue lacing to last set of holes on one side; leave tails of equal length at beginning and end of side. Remove lacing from needle.

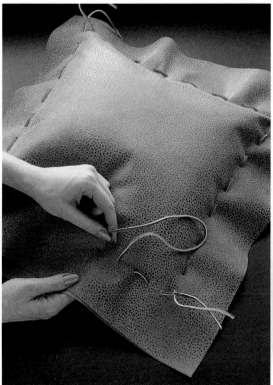

6 Repeat steps 3 to 5 for two more sides. Insert the pillow form into open side; lace the open side shut.

7 Lace tails through concho or button at corner, if desired; tie square knot. Repeat for all corners.

HOW TO MAKE A FRINGED PILLOW

MATERIALS

- Soft leather or suede, synthetic leather or suede, or reversible polyester fleece.
- Pillow form in desired size.
- Narrow masking tape.

CUTTING DIRECTIONS

Determine desired length of fringe; add 1½" (3.8 cm) for knots, if desired, on suede or leather. Cut pillow front and pillow back with sides equal to the measurements of the pillow form plus twice the length of the fringe, including allowance for knots.

1 Place the pillow front over the pillow back, wrong sides together, matching edges. Mark length of the fringe on all sides, using narrow masking tape. Mark desired width of fringe strips on tape, ½" (1.3 cm) for fleece, ⅜" to ½" (1 to 1.3 cm) for suede or leather. Secure layers together, using pins for fleece or paper clips for suede or leather. Sew three sides, using walking foot, if available.

2 Cut fringe on sewn sides, using rotary cutter and cutting board. Use straightedge as guide, cutting to within ½" (1.3 cm) of the tape. Finish cutting with the scissors up to, but not through, the stitching.

3 Insert pillow form; sew remaining side. Cut fringe on remaining side. Remove tape.

Optional knots. Grasp first set of fringe strips; tie together in overhand knot, securing knot tightly at stitching. Continue tying knots on all sides; for uniform appearance, tie all knots in the same direction.

MORE IDEAS FOR QUICK PILLOWS

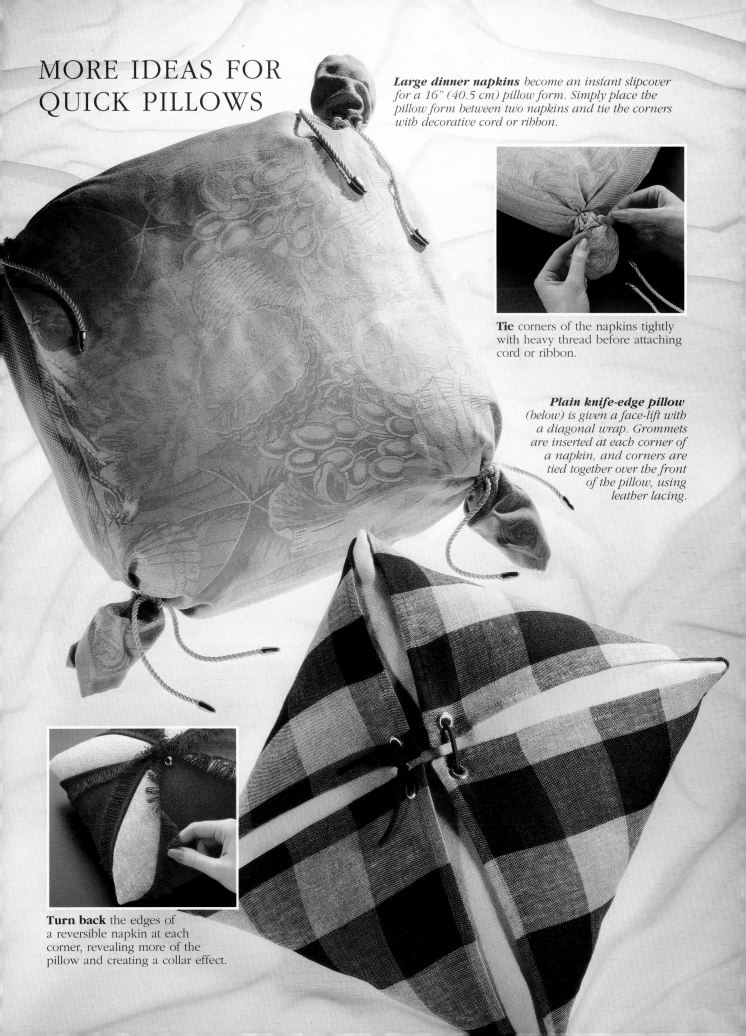

Large dinner napkins become an instant slipcover for a 16" (40.5 cm) pillow form. Simply place the pillow form between two napkins and tie the corners with decorative cord or ribbon.

Tie corners of the napkins tightly with heavy thread before attaching cord or ribbon.

Plain knife-edge pillow (below) is given a face-lift with a diagonal wrap. Grommets are inserted at each corner of a napkin, and corners are tied together over the front of the pillow, using leather lacing.

Turn back the edges of a reversible napkin at each corner, revealing more of the pillow and creating a collar effect.

TEXTURIZING TECHNIQUES
WITH PAINT

Plain painted walls can be revived quickly using painting techniques that give visual texture to the surface. Texturizing material is pressed into a thin layer of paint glaze and then imprinted repeatedly onto the wall. The first few imprints will be darker, releasing more of the glaze onto the wall. Each imprint releases a little less of the glaze, until only a shadow remains. This gradation in intensity gives the texturized wall dramatic depth.

Many different materials are suitable for texturizing, including crumpled paper, coarse fabric, a ball of string or twine, or coarse netting. Texturizing works best over a low-luster base coat. For a subtle effect, select a paint color that is slightly darker or lighter than the existing wall color. For a bolder effect, select a color with more contrast. Experiment with the color and technique before beginning the project.

MATERIALS

- Painter's masking tape; drop cloths.
- Latex or acrylic paint.
- Latex paint conditioner, such as Floetrol®.
- Water.
- Flat surface for glaze palette, such as paper plate; sponge applicator.
- Texturizing material, such as crumpled paper, coarse fabric, ball of string or twine, or coarse netting.

TEXTURIZING GLAZE RECIPE

Mix together the following ingredients:

One part latex or acrylic paint in desired color and sheen.

One part latex paint conditioner, such as Floetrol.

One part water.

HOW TO TEXTURIZE A WALL WITH PAINT

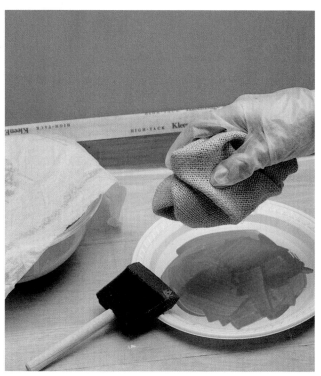

1 Mask off surrounding area, using painter's masking tape; protect the floor with drop cloths. Mix glaze, following recipe on page 43. Drape glaze container with wet cloth to keep glaze from drying out.

2 Spread a thin layer of glaze onto the palette, using a sponge applicator. Crumple or fold texturizing material as desired. Press the texturizing material into thin layer of glaze; lift.

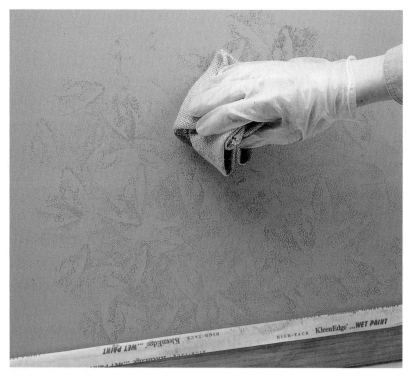

3 Imprint wall repeatedly with texturizing material, beginning in a lower corner; randomly cover an area about 24" × 24" (61 × 61 cm) in size, and rotate material at different angles with each imprinting motion, until all glaze is released onto wall.

4 Repeat steps 2 and 3, moving upward and outward on wall, until entire wall has been texturized; begin with fresh texturizing material as necessary.

TEXTURIZING EFFECTS

Coarse fabric. Fanfold a narrow length of burlap or other coarse fabric into a thick pad; flip folds to back of pad as they become saturated, exposing fresh fabric for texturizing **(a).** Or crumple a piece of coarse fabric into loose, irregular folds; recrumple or start with a fresh piece as fabric becomes saturated **(b).**

Paper. Crumple a sheet of firm paper into a loose wad of irregular folds. Discard paper and start with a fresh sheet as it becomes saturated.

Coarse netting. Netting balls, such as those found in bath shops, can be used for texturizing. Netting will not absorb the glaze, so will not become saturated.

Twine or string. To texturize with a distinctive pattern, use the twine or string as it comes in a ball, turning ball or unwinding twine or string as areas become saturated **(a).** Or, wind string or twine eratically into a tangle for more irregularly shaped pattern **(b).**

COLOR WASHING WALLS

Color washing is a fast way to give a plain painted wall a translucent, watercolored appearance. Purchase premixed color-washing solutions at paint or craft stores, or mix your own. Color washing works best if applied over a low-luster base coat. For subtle shading, select a color for the wash that is closely related to the wall color, in a darker or lighter tone. Soften a boldy painted wall with a neutral or white color wash. Or, if the wall color is neutral, select a color for the wash as desired.

Because the solution is very runny, it is important to mask off surrounding areas and cover the floor and furniture with waterproof drop cloths. Wear rubber gloves and old clothes, and keep an old towel nearby to wipe your hands as necessary.

COLOR-WASHING SOLUTION RECIPE

Mix together the following ingredients:

One part latex or acrylic paint.

Eight parts water.

HOW TO COLOR WASH WALLS

MATERIALS

- Painter's masking tape; drop cloths.
- Latex or acrylic paint; water, for mixing color-washing solution; or purchased color-washing solution.

- Paint pail.
- Large natural sea sponge.
- Rubber gloves; old towel.

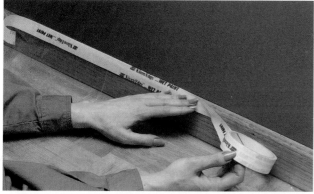

1 Mask off surrounding area, using painter's masking tape; protect floor with drop cloths. Mix color-washing solution, above, in paint pail, or pour purchased color-washing solution into pail.

2 Immerse sponge into color-washing solution. Lift the sponge; squeeze out excess solution, leaving sponge very wet.

3 Wipe color-washing solution onto wall in short, curved strokes, beginning in a lower corner; overlap and change directions of strokes, quickly covering an area of wall about 36" × 36" (91.5 × 91.5 cm). Add color to any bare areas by dabbing with the sponge.

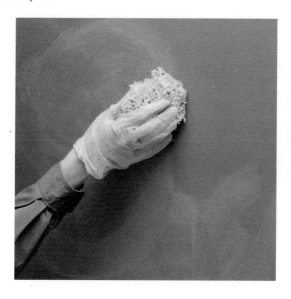

4 Repeat steps 2 and 3, moving upward and outward on wall until the entire wall has been color washed. Allow to dry thoroughly. If additional color is desired, apply a second coat.

Freehand painting is a speedy way to add eye-catching interest to plain painted walls. Designs can range from stately architectural details to fanciful motifs. Simple symmetrical designs in one color are easiest to paint, while asymmetrical designs or designs with multiple colors may take a little pre-planning. Use some of the designs shown here, or look for inspiration in wallpaper patterns, clip-art books, or stencils.

Craft acrylic paints or latex wall paints can be used for freehand painting. Acrylic paints, available in smaller quantities, may be more economical, depending on the size of the project. If a paint color is mixed, be sure to mix enough paint ahead of time to complete the entire project. Use wide, flat paintbrushes to paint bold lines; use other artist's brushes in styles and sizes necessary to achieve the desired look.

Allow the painted designs to be imperfect; that is part of the charm of free-hand painting. To gain confidence, practice designs on tagboard or craft paper taped to the wall with masking tape.

MATERIALS

- Craft acrylic paint or latex wall paint.
- Paintbrushes in desired sizes and styles.
- Masking tape; yardstick or carpenter's level, for marking guides as necessary.

Gold metallic design is painted on the wall at the head of the bed. Small fleur-de-lis motifs painted randomly on the walls support the decorating theme.

Symmetrically designed Greek columns painted on the wall visually support the shelf. The swag and tassel border is painted at picture-rail level.

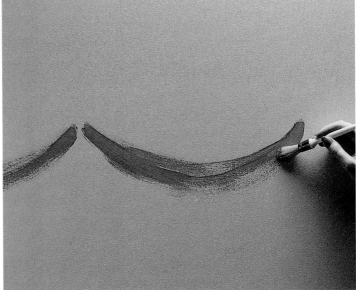

Borders. Mark guide points on wall, using yardstick or carpenter's level, before painting evenly spaced swags or wavy lines. Keep the brush moving at a constant, rhythmic pace across the wall, redipping brush in paint as necessary. Fill in details after entire border is laid out.

Symmetrical motifs (left). Paint the center of the design first; then paint small sections of the design on either side of the center, working outward until entire design is complete.

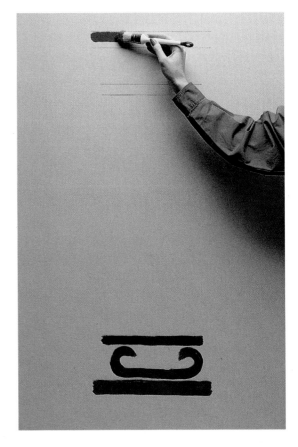

Random motifs. Mark placement for motifs, using small pieces of masking tape, before beginning to paint. Vary sizes or colors for added interest, if desired.

Large designs (right). Mark faint pencil guidelines on the wall at strategic points in large designs. Paint dominant details first to anchor design on wall; then paint secondary design lines to complete design.

MORE IDEAS FOR FREEHAND PAINTED DESIGNS

Faux brickwork *painted on the wall under a shelf resembles a fireplace and mantel. Faux brickwork chair rail continues around the room.*

Contemporary asymmetrical design *(above) painted on the wall boldly outlines a window. Small motifs taken from the design are painted randomly on the wall, unifying the room.*

CREATIVE WALL BORDERS

a

b

c

Wall borders can add instant detailing to a room and reinforce a decorating scheme. For a country kitchen, create a simple border with the use of garden seed packets. Or use decorative chain to border a rustic, lodge-style room.

Ribbon borders work well for a more traditional decor. Select a grosgrain ribbon embellished with decorative nails for a formal look. To dress up a girl's bedroom, add a ribbon-and-bows border positioned about 18" (46 cm) from the ceiling.

Corrugated cardboard can be used to create textural borders. They can be accented with shiny thumbtacks, decorative nails of antique brass, assorted buttons, or glass stones. For a more dimensional effect, art papers can be cut and folded to add occasional raised details along the border.

Borders can be positioned along the ceiling to draw the eye upward, providing a balance with lower elements in the room. Positioned at picture-rail level, 12" to 24" (30.5 to 61 cm) below the top of the wall, a border visually lowers the ceiling. To create other effects in the room, consider running the border around windows and doors, or place a border at chair-rail height, about one-third the distance up from the floor.

You may want to mark a placement guide on the walls for applying borders at chair-rail or picture-rail height. For borders that do not have to follow a straight line, such as randomly placed crayons, light pencil markings may be all you need as a placement guide. For a ribbon border, you may want to apply a straight line of painter's masking tape to the wall as on page 56.

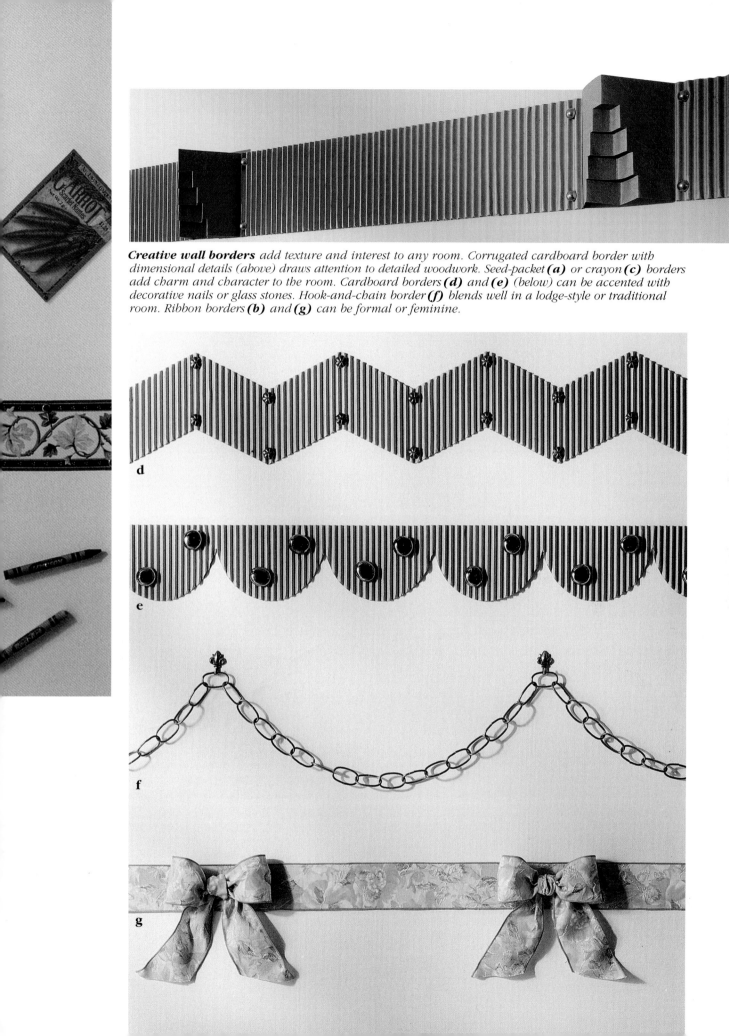

Creative wall borders *add texture and interest to any room. Corrugated cardboard border with dimensional details (above) draws attention to detailed woodwork. Seed-packet* ***(a)*** *or crayon* ***(c)*** *borders add charm and character to the room. Cardboard borders* ***(d)*** *and* ***(e)*** *(below) can be accented with decorative nails or glass stones. Hook-and-chain border* ***(f)*** *blends well in a lodge-style or traditional room. Ribbon borders* ***(b)*** *and* ***(g)*** *can be formal or feminine.*

d

e

f

g

HOW TO MAKE A CORRUGATED CARDBOARD BORDER
WITH DECORATIVE NAILS

MATERIALS

• Single-face corrugated cardboard, available at art supply stores.

• Decorative nails or tacks.

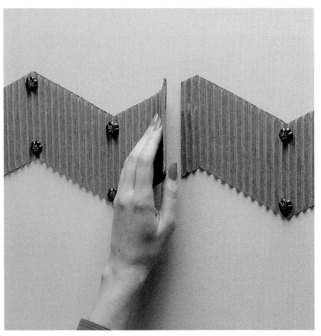

1 Cut corrugated cardboard into strips of desired width, cutting across the ribs in the cardboard. Cut the strips straight across or in a scalloped or zigzag design; use a template for accuracy, if desired.

2 Attach strips to wall, using a decorative nail or tack at upper and lower edges of strip; overlap ends of strips as shown, tacking through both layers. Apply additional nails as desired, for embellishment.

HOW TO MAKE A CORRUGATED CARDBOARD BORDER
WITH GLASS STONES OR BUTTONS

MATERIALS

• Single-face corrugated cardboard, available at art supply stores.

• Glass stones or buttons.

• Hot glue gun and glue sticks.

• Thumbtacks.

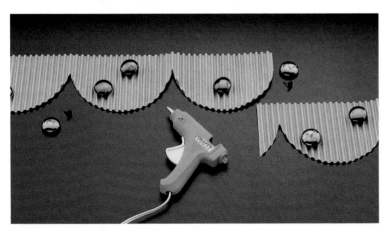

1 Cut corrugated cardboard as in step 1, above. Apply glass stones or buttons to cardboard randomly, using hot glue; allow space at center and ends of strips for stones or buttons that will be placed over tacks at overlaps.

2 Attach strips to wall with thumbtacks as in step 2, above. Apply glass stones or buttons over tacks, using hot glue.

HOW TO MAKE A CORRUGATED CARDBOARD BORDER
WITH DIMENSIONAL DETAILS

MATERIALS

- Single-face corrugated cardboard.
- Art paper.
- Decorative nails or tacks.

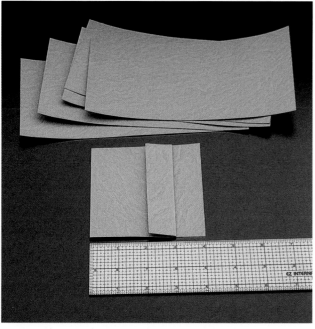

1 Cut a 4" × 8" (10 × 20.5 cm) piece of art paper. Fold in half, to make a folded 4" (10 cm) square. Fold back 1" (2.5 cm) at each end.

2 Cut four slits, evenly spaced, along the center fold, decreasing the length of each slit.

3 Unfold paper. Crease paper vertically at ends of slits, folding paper in opposite direction from center fold.

4 Cut corrugated cardboard into 4" (10 cm) strips, cutting across the ribs in the cardboard. Attach the border to wall as for border with decorative nails, step 2, opposite; use decorative nails or tacks to secure dimensional details at ends of cardboard sections, tucking 1" (2.5 cm) ends of details under cardboard.

DECORATING THE WALLS

HOW TO MAKE A RIBBON BORDER

MATERIALS

- Decorative ribbon.
- Carpenter's level; masking tape.
- Decorative nails or thumbtacks.
- Hot glue gun and glue sticks, for ribbon border with bows.

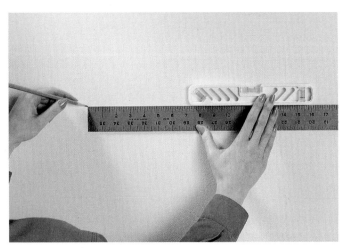

1 Mark the wall with light pencil markings at 36" to 48" (91.5 to 122 cm) intervals, using a carpenter's level.

2 Stretch masking tape straight across between markings, as a placement guide. Attach ribbon to wall with one edge of ribbon along edge of tape; secure ribbon with decorative nails at evenly spaced intervals along upper and lower edges of ribbon. Remove tape.

HOW TO MAKE A HOOK & CHAIN BORDER

MATERIALS

- Decorative chain.
- Pushpin hangers.

1 Attach pushpin hangers to wall, spacing them evenly about 18" (46 cm) apart; begin and end at corners of wall.

2 Hang the chain on hangers, allowing chain to drape equally between the hangers.

Ribbon border with bows. Follow steps 1 and 2 for ribbon border, opposite, using thumbtacks to secure ribbon to wall; place thumbtacks at evenly spaced intervals along center of ribbon. Cut additional ribbon into 24" (61 cm) lengths, and tie into bows. Attach bows over thumbtacks, using hot glue.

HOW TO MAKE A CRAYON OR SEED-PACKET BORDER

MATERIALS

- Crayons and #18 × ½" (1.3 cm) escutcheon pins, for crayon border.

- Seed packets and copper weather-strip nails, for seed-packet border.

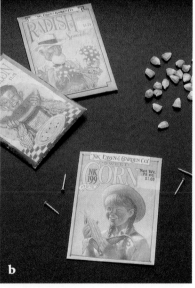

1 Push escutcheon pin gently through center of each crayon **(a).** Or apply copper weather-strip nails to corners of seed packets **(b);** seeds may be removed, if desired, by cutting a small slit in back of packet.

2 Apply crayons or seed packets to wall in a randomly spaced border design.

RIBBON-FRAMED WALLS

Ribbon frames instantly divide a plain wall into sections, giving the illusion of architectural detail. Tall, narrow ribbon frames add visual height to a wall, while wide, stacked ribbon frames make the wall seem wider and shorter. You may want to use a ribbon frame to outline a wall arrangement or emphasize existing wall divisions.

A few minutes taken for accurate measuring and planning make installation of the ribbon frames a breeze. Sketching the wall and ribbon frames to scale on graph paper allows you to visualize the end result, eliminating time-consuming guesswork during installation.

Purchase grosgrain ribbon in the desired width, from 3⁄8" to 11⁄2" (1 to 3.8 cm) wide. If the entire length needed for one frame cannot be purchased in one continuous piece, plan to join the pieces at the corners. Secure the ribbon to the wall at the frame corners and along the sides, using decorative upholstery tacks. For ribbon 7⁄8" (2.2 cm) wide or wider, two tacks may be preferred at each corner and at each tacking site along the sides. To save time, visually estimate the spacing between the tacking sites; if more accuracy is preferred, use a tape measure.

MATERIALS

- Tape measure.
- Graph paper.
- Decorative upholstery tacks; tack hammer.
- Masking tape.
- Grosgrain ribbon in desired width, from 3⁄8" to 11⁄2" (1 to 3.8 cm); length determined after drawing plan to scale in step 1 on page 60.

CUTTING DIRECTIONS

For the continuous method, cut one piece of ribbon with the length equal to the distance around the frame plus 3" (7.5 cm). For the pieced method, cut four pieces of ribbon with the length of each piece equal to the length of one side plus 3" (7.5 cm).

HOW TO INSTALL A RIBBON FRAME ON A WALL
(CONTINUOUS METHOD)

1 Measure the wall accurately; draw the wall to scale on graph paper, including doors, windows, or fixtures. Determine the desired size and placement of ribbon frames; draw frames to scale, indicating measurements of all sides. Mark the placement of frame corners on the wall, using graphed drawing as guide.

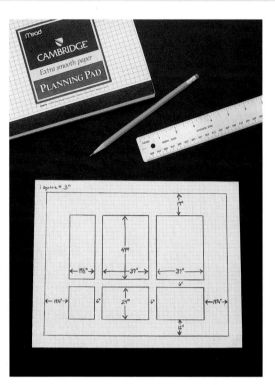

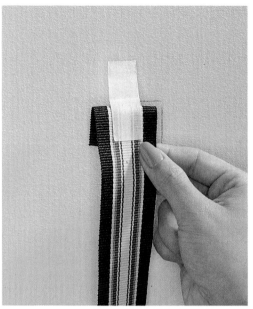

2 Fold under end of the ribbon 1" (2.5 cm). Align the outer corner of folded end to a marked frame corner. Secure the ribbon end to the wall, using masking tape.

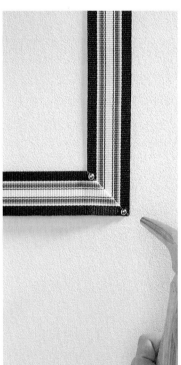

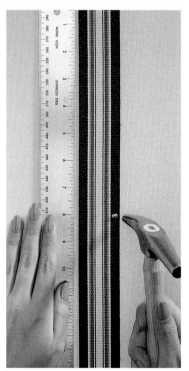

3 Pull ribbon taut to the next marked corner; miter ribbon so that point of mitered corner aligns to mark. Tack the mitered corner to wall, inserting one or two tacks through fold.

4 Repeat step 3 for next two marked corners. Pull ribbon taut to taped corner. Fold end of ribbon back diagonally, aligning point of fold to outer corner of the frame; trim excess ribbon. Remove tape holding straight folded end; place diagonally folded end over straight end, and tack in place.

5 Secure ribbon to wall along each side of the frame, using additional upholstery tacks; space tacks as desired, estimating or measuring distances.

HOW TO INSTALL A RIBBON FRAME ON A WALL
(PIECED METHOD)

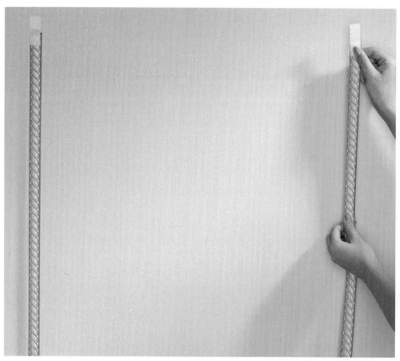

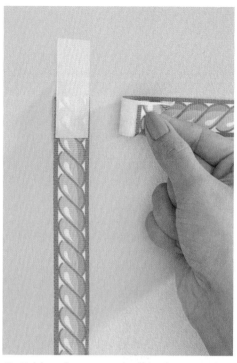

1 Follow step 1 (opposite). Fold under one end of a vertical ribbon piece 1" (2.5 cm); tape to wall, aligning outer corner of folded end to upper marked corner. Pull ribbon taut to mark for lower corner. Fold under ribbon even with mark; trim excess to 1" (2.5 cm). Tape in place. Repeat for opposite side.

2 Fold under one end of the horizontal ribbon piece diagonally. Remove tape holding end of vertical piece; lap diagonally folded end over straight end, and tack in place, using one or two tacks.

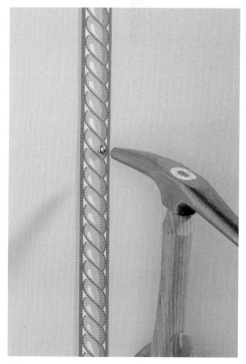

3 Pull ribbon taut to opposite corner. Fold end diagonally so that point of diagonal fold aligns to marked corner; trim excess ribbon. Remove tape; lap diagonally folded end over straight end, and tack in place.

4 Repeat steps 2 and 3 for remaining side of frame. Complete the frame, following step 5 (opposite).

MORE IDEAS FOR RIBBON FRAMES

Double ribbon frame
(above), made with two
different widths of ribbon,
outlines a collection of
awards and photographs
in a child's bedroom.

Ribbon frames (opposite)
on the lower section of this
wall emphasize the existing
wainscoting.

**Tall, narrow ribbon
frames** (right) add visual
height to the room.

Floral Accents

EASY GRAPEVINE WREATHS

Make eye-catching wreaths to enhance any decorating style, using simple grapevine wreaths and artificial floral material. Embellish a wreath with silk ivy garlands for instant freshness. Attach lush stems of latex fruits and berries, complete with leaves and curly vines. For a woodsy effect, create a focal point on a grapevine wreath by clustering assorted bird's nests. To make a blooming wreath, purchase silk blooming plants, which are more economical and have more leaves than individual flower stems. Secure all embellishments to the grapevine wreath quickly and easily, using a hot glue gun or floral wire.

MATERIALS

- Grapevine wreath.
- Hot glue gun and glue sticks; floral wire.
- Silk ivy garland, large-leafed stems, raffia, for foliage wreath.

- Stems of latex fruit and berries with leaves and curly vines, 1 yd. to 2 yd. (0.95 to 1.85 m) ribbon, optional, for wreath with fruit and berries.
- Bird's nests in assorted shapes and sizes, dried baby's breath, for wreath with clustered nests.
- Silk blooming plants, wire cutter, 2½ yd. to 3 yd. (2.3 to 2.75 m) ribbon, for blooming wreath.

HOW TO MAKE A FOLIAGE WREATH

1 Wrap ivy garland around grapevine wreath; secure, using hot glue as needed.

2 Cut single leaves from large-leafed stems. Arrange leaves throughout wreath as desired; secure, using hot glue.

3 Tie several strands of raffia into bow with long tails; secure to top of wreath, using floral wire or hot glue.

HOW TO MAKE A WREATH WITH FRUIT & BERRIES

1 Arrange several stems of fruit and berries around the grapevine wreath, inserting stems into the wreath and clustering them more heavily in one area to create a focal point; secure, using hot glue.

2 Weave a ribbon around the wreath, if desired, arranging twists and loops; secure with hot glue as necessary.

HOW TO MAKE A WREATH WITH CLUSTERED NESTS

1 Arrange bird's nests in cluster near center of grapevine wreath; secure, using floral wire or hot glue.

2 Apply hot glue to sprigs of baby's breath; insert into grapevine and around nests for accent.

HOW TO MAKE A BLOOMING WREATH

1 Cut flower stems from silk blooming plant. Arrange flowers evenly around wreath, inserting stems into wreath; secure, using hot glue.

2 Cut leafy stems from plant. Fill in areas around flowers with leaves, inserting stems into wreath; secure, using hot glue.

3 Make cluster bow with long tails (below). Secure bow to wreath, using floral wire. Trail tails of bow through flowers and leaves, securing as necessary.

HOW TO MAKE A CLUSTER BOW

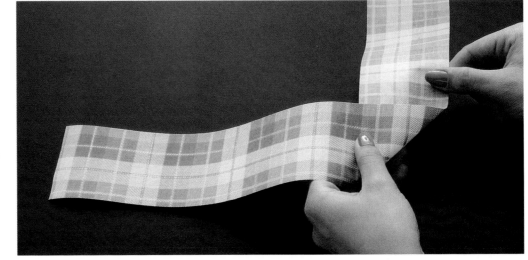

1 Place thumb and index finger at determined length for tail, with the ribbon right side up. Fold ribbon back on itself at a diagonal, with wrong sides together, so ribbon forms a right angle.

2 Wrap ribbon over thumb to form center loop; secure with fingers. Twist the ribbon one-half turn at underside of loop, so right side of the ribbon faces up.

3 Form first loop. Twist ribbon one-half turn, and form loop on opposite side.

4 Continue forming loops under the previous loops, alternating sides and twisting the ribbon so the right side always faces up; make each loop slightly larger than the loop above it.

5 When final loop has been formed, insert wire through center of bow. Bend wire around ribbon at center; twist wire tightly, gathering ribbon. Hold wire firmly at the top, and turn the bow, twisting wire snug. Separate and shape the loops.

Eye-catching containers for fresh flowers can be made in an instant, using discarded cans. Disguised in wraps of various craft materials, empty cans that might otherwise be thrown away can be recycled artistically. Birch bark may be wrapped around a can and embellished with bits of moss or twigs for a woodsy vase. Or an empty can might become a flower basket, using moss, twigs, and raffia. Birch bark may be cut from firewood or fallen trees or purchased at floral supply stores.

MATERIALS

- Empty can in desired size.
- Birch bark, removed from firewood or fallen trees (page 103).
- Utility knife or craft scissors.
- Hot glue gun and glue sticks.
- Fresh sheet moss.
- Embellishments, such as twigs or jute rope.

HOW TO MAKE A BIRCH-BARK VASE

1 Cut birch bark with measurements equal to the height and circumference of the can, using utility knife. Glue bark to can, using hot glue gun.

2 Embellish with twigs or jute rope as desired, covering butted seams of bark.

3 Cut a strip of fresh sheet moss about 2" (5 cm) wide, with the length equal to the circumference of the can. Glue to upper edge, lapping over rim of can. Glue 1" (2.5 cm) strip to lower edge.

4 Bend a section of chicken wire into a mounded form and insert into container. Fill vase with fresh flowers, using wire form to keep flower stems in place.

HOW TO MAKE A MOSS-WRAPPED FLOWER BASKET

MATERIALS

- Empty can in desired size.
- Fresh sheet moss.
- Hot glue gun and glue sticks.

- Freshly cut straight twigs for handle, ¼" to ½" (6 mm to 1.3 cm) in diameter, in desired length.
- Green florist's wire.
- Raffia.

1 Cover outside of can with fresh sheet moss, using hot glue gun; lap moss over upper edge of can.

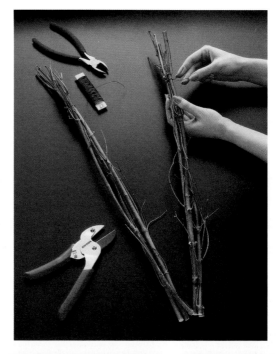

2 Cut six to eight twigs with lengths approximately three times the height of the can, staggering lengths slightly. Form the twigs into two bundles, with thicker ends of the twigs aligned at lower ends of the bundles; secure bundles with florist's wire near lower ends and again near upper ends.

3 Stand bundles on opposite sides of the can, with lower ends of the bundles even with the bottom of can. Secure bundles to can with florist's wire, wrapping wire around can and twigs near the upper edge and again near the lower edge.

4 Make a short bundle of twigs with slightly staggered lengths about 3" (7.5 cm) longer than diameter of can. Place the short bundle crosswise over long bundles near upper ends; wire in place, forming handle.

5 Tie raffia around joints of handle, covering wire. Wrap raffia around flower basket, covering wire near upper edge of can; tie bow, leaving long tails. Follow step 4 on page 73.

MORE IDEAS FOR FRESH FLOWER CONTAINERS

Recycled wide-mouthed jar studded with gemstones becomes a stunning vase.

Affix embellishments to glass jars and bottles, using small amounts of silicone glue and following the manufacturer's instructions.

Rejuvenated bottles, adorned with flat stones or seashells, make stylish bud vases.

SINGLE-VARIETY ARRANGEMENTS

When time is limited, the easiest way to create an impressive floral arrangement is to use elements of a single variety. A bouquet of flowers, all of the same variety and color, is much easier to arrange than a mixed bouquet. Whether you are using fresh, silk, or dried flowers, the uniformity of shape and color creates bold impact. Two or three items of a contrasting color or variety may be added as an accent.

Fresh flowers can be arranged in a glass vase, using a grid of clear waterproof floral tape over the mouth of the vase to keep the stems in place. Or floral foam designed for fresh flowers can be secured to the bottom of any waterproof container to hold the flower stems.

Silk and dried flowers are arranged by inserting the stems into the appropriate type of floral foam. Floral foam designed for dried flowers is softer than that designed for silk flowers, because the stems of dried material are more fragile.

MATERIALS

- Container.
- Floral foam; select type of foam appropriate for fresh, silk, or dried flowers.
- Clear waterproof floral tape, for fresh flower arrangement.
- Sheet moss or Spanish moss, anchor pin, floral pins, floral adhesive clay, for silk or dried arrangement.
- Potpourri, marbles, small pine-cones, or other desired material, for silk or dried arrangement in glass container.
- Flower stems of single variety; fresh, silk, or dried.
- Sharp knife.
- Cut-flower food, for fresh flower arrangement.

HOW TO PREPARE THE CONTAINER
FOR A FRESH FLORAL ARRANGEMENT

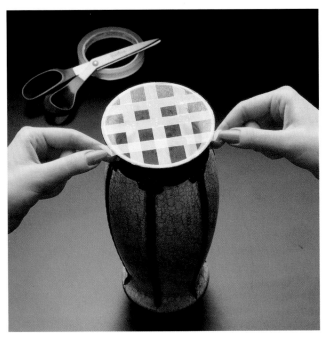

Floral tape grid. Make a grid over the mouth of the container, using waterproof floral tape. Add water containing cut-flower food to two-thirds full.

1 Floral foam. Select floral foam appropriate for fresh flower arranging. Soak the foam in water containing cut-flower food for at least 20 minutes.

HOW TO MAKE A SINGLE-VARIETY FRESH ARRANGEMENT

1 Prepare container (above). Cut flower stems at an angle to desired heights, cutting at least 1" (2.5 cm) above original cut; for roses, cut stems at an angle while submerging them in water.

2 Remove any leaves that will be covered by water in finished arrangement; leaves left in water will shorten life of arrangement.

2 Cut foam, using a knife, so it fits container and extends about 1" (2.5 cm) above rim. Round off upper edges of foam, if necessary, to prevent foam from showing in finished arrangement. Secure with waterproof tape.

3 Floral tape grid. Insert the flower stems into container and arrange as desired, using floral tape grid to support stems of flowers. Add water as necessary.

3 Floral foam. Insert the flowers into the foam, spacing evenly around the container and varying heights as desired. Allow flowers around edges of container to drape slightly downward, hiding foam.

HOW TO PREPARE THE CONTAINER
FOR A SILK OR DRIED ARRANGEMENT

1 **Opaque container.** Select appropriate floral foam for silk or dried arrangement. Cut foam, using knife, so it fits the container snugly and is ½" to ¾" (1.3 to 2 cm) below the rim for vertical arrangement **(a)**, or extends about 1" (2.5 cm) above container for horizontal or draping arrangement **(b).** Cut and insert wedges of foam as necessary; round off the top edges of foam to prevent foam from showing in finished arrangement.

2 Cover foam lightly with moss, securing it with floral pins, if necessary.

HOW TO MAKE A HORIZONTAL
OR DRAPING SILK ARRANGEMENT

1 Prepare container (above). Insert stems of silk flowers into foam, spacing evenly around container and varying heights as desired. Bend stems slightly downward near outer edges, draping flowers for natural appearance.

1 **Glass container.** Cut block of appropriate foam so it can be inserted into the center of the container with space around all sides. Apply floral adhesive clay to the bottom of the anchor pin; secure to the bottom of glass container. Press foam firmly onto prongs of the anchor pin.

2 Fill surrounding area with potpourri, marbles, small pinecones, or other desired material.

HOW TO MAKE A VERTICAL SINGLE-VARIETY DRIED ARRANGEMENT

1 Prepare the container (above). Insert the stems of dried flowers vertically into the foam, starting in the center and working out in a circle until desired fullness is achieved. Stems in outer rows may be shorter than those in the center.

DRIED FLORAL ARRANGEMENTS

Create a dried floral arrangement to bring color and softness into a room in a matter of minutes. The spiral assembly method requires no preplanning and eliminates time-consuming guesswork or repositioning of materials.

Select dried filler material consisting of small flowers or foliage, in an assortment of textures. Accent materials are slightly larger in size than the filler materials and have distinctive shapes. Follow a color scheme to complement or contrast with the colors in the room.

HOW TO MAKE A DRIED FLORAL ARRANGEMENT

MATERIALS

- Container.
- Floral foam for dried flowers; knife.

- Three or more varieties of dried filler material, such as heather, rushes, leptosporum, or caspia.

- Two varieties of dried accent material, such as roses, wheat, Billy buttons, or strawflowers.

1 Cut the foam, using knife, so it fits container snugly and extends about 1" (2.5 cm) above container. Round off upper edges of foam.

2 Insert one stem of filler material into center of foam, establishing the height of arrangement about 10" (25.5 cm) above container. Insert other stems of filler material in circle around the center, alternating varieties.

3 Continue inserting filler material in spiral pattern, from center outward, alternating the varieties of materials. Shorten stems slightly with each row and gradually change the angle of insertion, forming rounded shape; stems at outer row of arrangement should be 2" to 3" (5 to 7.5 cm) long.

4 Insert accent materials into foam, spacing them evenly throughout the arrangement and inserting them at same height and angle as the surrounding material.

QUICK FLORAL DISPLAYS

Floral displays placed on top of cabinets, such as armoires and entertainment centers, can add the finishing touch to a room's decor. These artful arrangements of floral items are quick to assemble. The easy step-by-step instructions on the following pages eliminate the guesswork and planning normally involved in making a floral arrangement.

Potted silk plants and latex fruit (top) are combined in an artful display.

Assorted wreaths (bottom left) are accented with a silk arrangement for a woodsy display.

Interesting found objects (bottom right) are arranged in a theme display.

HOW TO MAKE A DISPLAY OF POTTED PLANTS

MATERIALS

- Clay pots in several sizes.
- Silk plants, including one trailing plant, such as ivy.
- Burgundy eucalyptus.

- Latex grapes or other clusters of artificial fruit.
- Floral Styrofoam®.
- Honeysuckle vines, optional.

1 Place clay pots of various sizes on display surface with largest pot off center, surrounded by two or three medium-size pots. Fill in the display area with two or more smaller pots, turning one on its side.

2 Place pieces of green floral Styrofoam inside large pot. Place additional pieces of Styrofoam inside smaller, upturned pots.

3 Cut stems from silk green plants. Insert ends of stems into the Styrofoam pieces inside the pots, to create potted plants, curving some of the stems downward over the sides of the pots.

4 Place additional cut stems around pots; concentrate more stems in the center display area. Drape some stems down over sides and front of display cabinet.

5 Intersperse clustered stems of burgundy eucalyptus among the greens; insert stems into foam to secure them.

6 Add a few clusters of latex grapes, with some of the clusters resting on the rims of the pots and draped over the edges.

7 Add honeysuckle vines, if desired, distributing the vines randomly throughout the arrangement.

HOW TO MAKE A DISPLAY OF WREATHS

MATERIALS

- Wreaths made from various materials, such as twig, grapevine, and honeysuckle, and in various sizes.

- Silk ivy plant.
- Silk arrangement, decorative accessory, optional.

1 Lean three large or medium-size wreaths against the wall; use wreaths made from different materials, such as twig, grapevine, and honeysuckle.

2 Lean wreaths in varying sizes against the background wreaths, layering them; stack a few of the smaller wreaths in front.

3 Add a silk arrangement or decorative accessory to the display, if desired.

4 Cut stems from silk ivy plant. Arrange the stems through and around the wreaths, creating a wispy look.

HOW TO MAKE A DISPLAY WITH FOUND OBJECTS

MATERIALS

- Several found objects, such as crates, shutters, baskets, or wagons.
- Excelsior or a piece of gingham.

- Bundles of dried flowers.
- Baby's breath.
- Vintage or new garden tools.

1 Place a crate, wagon, or other interesting container on display surface, to the left of center and positioned at slight angle. Lean taller objects against the wall. Place a basket to the right of the first item.

2 Place a bed of excelsior or a piece of gingham in the crate or wagon, draping it over the side.

3 Place bundles of dried flowers in the crate, over the excelsior or gingham. Fill the basket with baby's breath.

4 Embellish the display with garden tools, if desired.

Creative
Accessories

SPRAY PAINTING TECHNIQUES

Spray paint, available in a wide range of colors and finishes, can be used to give a new look to old furniture and accessories. Application of spray paint results in a smooth surface, is much faster than brushing, and drying time is relatively short. Proper preparation of the surface to be painted and masking off of the area adjacent to it will ensure success of the project and make cleanup time minimal. Carefully follow the spray paint manufacturer's instructions. Always use spray paints in well-ventilated areas and avoid inhaling the fumes.

Apply several thin coats of spray paint, allowing the paint to dry between coats, for a smooth finish without runs. Hold the can 10" to 12" (25.5 to 30.5 cm) from the surface, continually moving in a sweeping motion. Turn the can upside down and spray for several seconds to clean the nozzle after each application.

SPRAY PAINTING TIPS

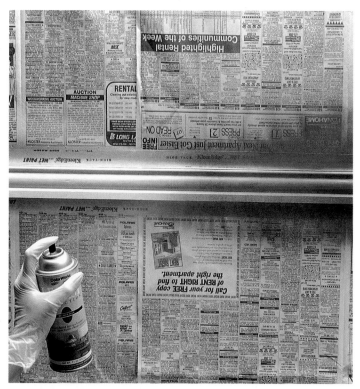

Mask off adjacent wall areas, using masking tape and newspaper and covering a wide area, to prevent overspray.

Place small items to be spray painted into a large box turned on its side. Spray into the box, avoiding overspray.

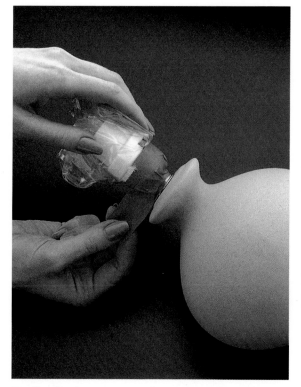

Mask off adjacent areas of an accessory, using masking tape and plastic bags.

Prop the item to be spray painted on a base, such as an empty narrow-necked bottle. Turn the item as necessary to cover the entire item with each coat.

Tray (above) is adorned with leaf silhouettes, using an easy spray painting technique. A fine mist of metallic spray paint adds sparkle to a pair of candlesticks (above). Glazed pottery vase (above) is given a spattered finish with spray paint. The stenciled design on the chair back and the antiqued finish on the basket (left) were both applied with spray paint.

SPECIAL EFFECTS
WITH SPRAY PAINT

Create special decorative effects quickly with spray paint. Using a timesaving spray painting technique, stencil a design in a flash. Create a silhouette by spraying over a leaf or a doily, leaving its image on the surface when it is removed. Add visual depth to a painted surface by specking with a dark spray paint. Give an old finish new luster with metallic shading, or instantly antique a new finish with a wood-tone spray paint.

HOW TO STENCIL WITH SPRAY PAINT

MATERIALS

- Precut stencil.
- Spray adhesive.
- Masking tape, newspaper for masking area adjacent to design.
- Spray paint.

1 Apply newspaper strips, about 20" (51 cm) wide, to outer edges of stencil plates, using masking tape. Apply spray adhesive to the back of stencil plates.

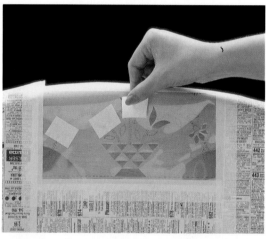

2 Position first stencil plate; press firmly to the surface to affix. Secure outer edges of newspaper with masking tape, if necessary. Mask off openings as necessary if more than one color will be applied using first plate.

3 Spray very lightly; allow to dry. Repeat. Remove tape from any masked-off openings; mask off painted openings. Spray second color; allow to dry.

4 Remove first stencil plate. Repeat steps 2 and 3 for additional stencil plates, matching the design with each plate placement.

HOW TO CREATE A SILHOUETTE WITH SPRAY PAINT

MATERIALS

- Flat object for silhouette image, such as a paper doily, fern leaf, or lace trim.
- Spray adhesive.
- Spray paint.

1 Apply spray adhesive to back of flat object. Affix to the surface.

2 Spray the entire surface evenly; apply several light coats, allowing the surface to dry between coats. Remove object, revealing silhouette.

INSTANT EFFECTS WITH SPRAY PAINT

Metallic shading. Select gold or copper spray paint for a warm glow, or silver spray paint for a cool, contemporary look. Spray metallic paint lightly and quickly over surface, holding can 20" to 26" (51 to 66 cm) from surface. Allow first fine coat to dry. Apply additional fine coats, if desired.

Specking. Depress the spray nozzle very lightly so that tiny droplets of paint come out and create specks on the surface. Practice this technique before applying it to the intended surface, to learn how far to depress the nozzle.

Instant antiquing. Select a wood-tone floral spray paint. Spray lightly and quickly over the surface for a translucent effect.

MORE SPECIAL EFFECTS WITH SPRAY PAINT

Faux stone finish (near right) is created instantly, using a specially designed spray paint. Pearlescent finish (far right) is achieved by spraying a painted surface with pearl glaze.

Crackled finish (below) is created in one step with a uniquely designed spray paint, available in a variety of colors.

COPPER FOIL
PICTURE FRAMES

Copper foil tape, available at stained glass supply stores, is used to make these quick and creative picture frames. The artwork or photograph is encased between mat board and glass and sealed at the edges with the copper foil tape. Pressure between layers keeps the artwork or photograph from sliding out of position.

The mat board may be used simply as a backing for the project when no margin is desired around the artwork or photograph, such as with children's paintings or classic advertising art. When a margin is desired, choose a mat board that will complement or set off the artwork or photograph; cut the glass and mat board larger to allow for the desired margin of mat board to show. As another alternative, use a

second piece of glass for the backing instead of the mat board, thus allowing the artwork or photograph to seemingly float in air.

Glass can be cut to size at the store, or you can cut it yourself, following steps 1 to 6 on page 100. Safety glasses are recommended whenever you are cutting glass, to protect your eyes from flying glass splinters. Clean up the work surface with a hand broom after cutting glass; never brush the surface with your hand.

Adhesive hangers may be applied to the back of the framed project for hanging on the wall. For display on a shelf or table, the framed project may be supported on a plate stand or small easel.

HOW TO MAKE A COPPER FOIL PICTURE FRAME

MATERIALS

- Artwork or photograph to be framed.
- Single-strength glass and tools for cutting glass, as listed on page 100.
- Mat board.
- Mat knife.
- Binder clips.
- 3/8" (1 cm) or 1/2" (1.3 cm) copper foil tape.
- Wooden craft stick.
- Self-adhesive picture hanger, for hanging on wall.
- Plate stand or small easel, for free-standing display.

CUTTING DIRECTIONS

Cut the glass to the desired finished size, following steps 1 to 6 on pages 100 and 101. Cut one piece for a frame with mat board backing; cut two pieces for a frame with glass backing. For a frame with mat board backing, cut the mat board to the same size as the glass, using a mat knife.

Cut a length of foil tape to the exact measurement of each side of the glass.

1 Frame with mat board backing. Place artwork or photograph faceup on right side of mat board backing in desired position. Clean both sides of glass thoroughly; place glass over artwork or photograph, aligning edges to backing. Clamp the layers together, using binder clips.

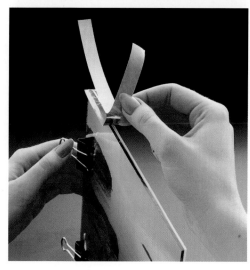

2 Peel about 2" (5 cm) of protective backing from one length of foil tape; remove the binder clips along corresponding side. Apply foil tape to outer edge, centering tape over backing and glass so equal amounts will wrap to the front and back. Continue to remove backing as tape is applied.

3 Fold edges of copper foil tape to front and back. Smooth edges of tape firmly, using wooden craft stick, to ease out any bubbles or gaps.

(Continued)

HOW TO MAKE A COPPER FOIL PICTURE FRAME (CONTINUED)

4 Repeat steps 2 and 3 for remaining sides, beginning with side opposite the first side. Attach self-adhesive picture hanger to back of frame, if desired.

Frame with glass backing. Follow steps 1 to 4 on pages 99 and 100, using glass backing instead of mat board. Mark placement of artwork on back side of glass backing, using narrow tape.

HOW TO CUT GLASS

MATERIALS

- Single-strength glass.
- Fine-tip marking pen; cork-backed straightedge.
- Glass cutter.
- Grozing pliers.

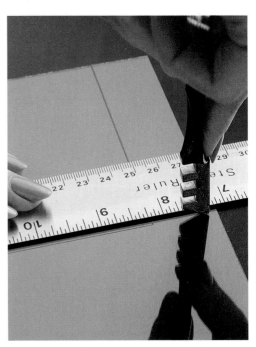

1 Mark cutting lines on glass, using fine-tip marking pen and cork-backed straightedge. Use outer edges of glass sheet as one or two sides whenever possible. Place straightedge along one marked line on glass, from one edge of glass sheet completely across to the opposite edge. Check to see that the wheel of the glass cutter (arrow) will line up exactly on marked line.

2 Hold the glass cutter perpendicular to the glass, with the wheel parallel to the straightedge, beginning ⅛" (3 mm) from one edge of the glass. Hold the straightedge firmly in place with the other hand.

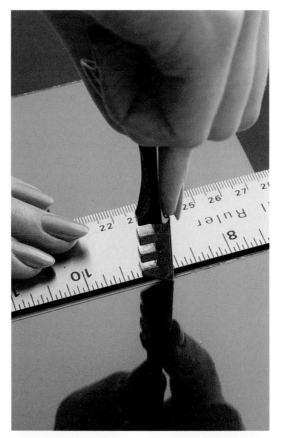

3 Push or pull the glass cutter, depending on which is more comfortable for you, across the glass from edge to edge, to score the glass; exert firm pressure, maintain constant speed, and keep the cutter perpendicular to the glass. Ease up on the pressure as you score off the glass on the opposite edge. Score the glass only once; do not repeat the process.

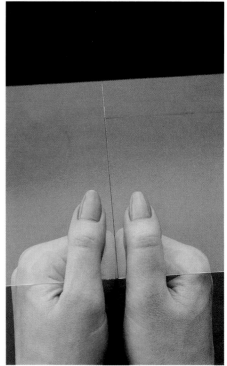

4 Hold the glass in both hands with the scored line between your thumbs; curl your fingers under the glass, making fists, with knuckles touching each other.

5 Apply quick, even pressure as you roll your thumbs out from each other, turning your wrists upward; this breaks the glass along the scored line.

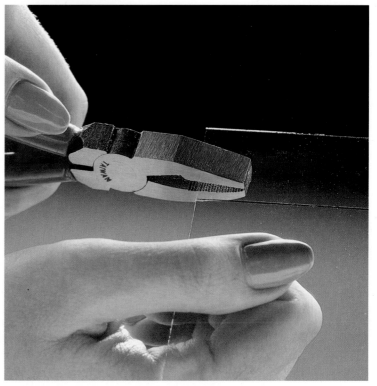

6 Repeat steps 2 to 5 for each remaining line marked on the glass. If the glass is not wide enough to grasp safely or effectively with your fingers, use grozing pliers, holding the pliers at a right angle close to the end of the score, with the flat jaw of the pliers on top of the glass.

RUSTIC FRAMES

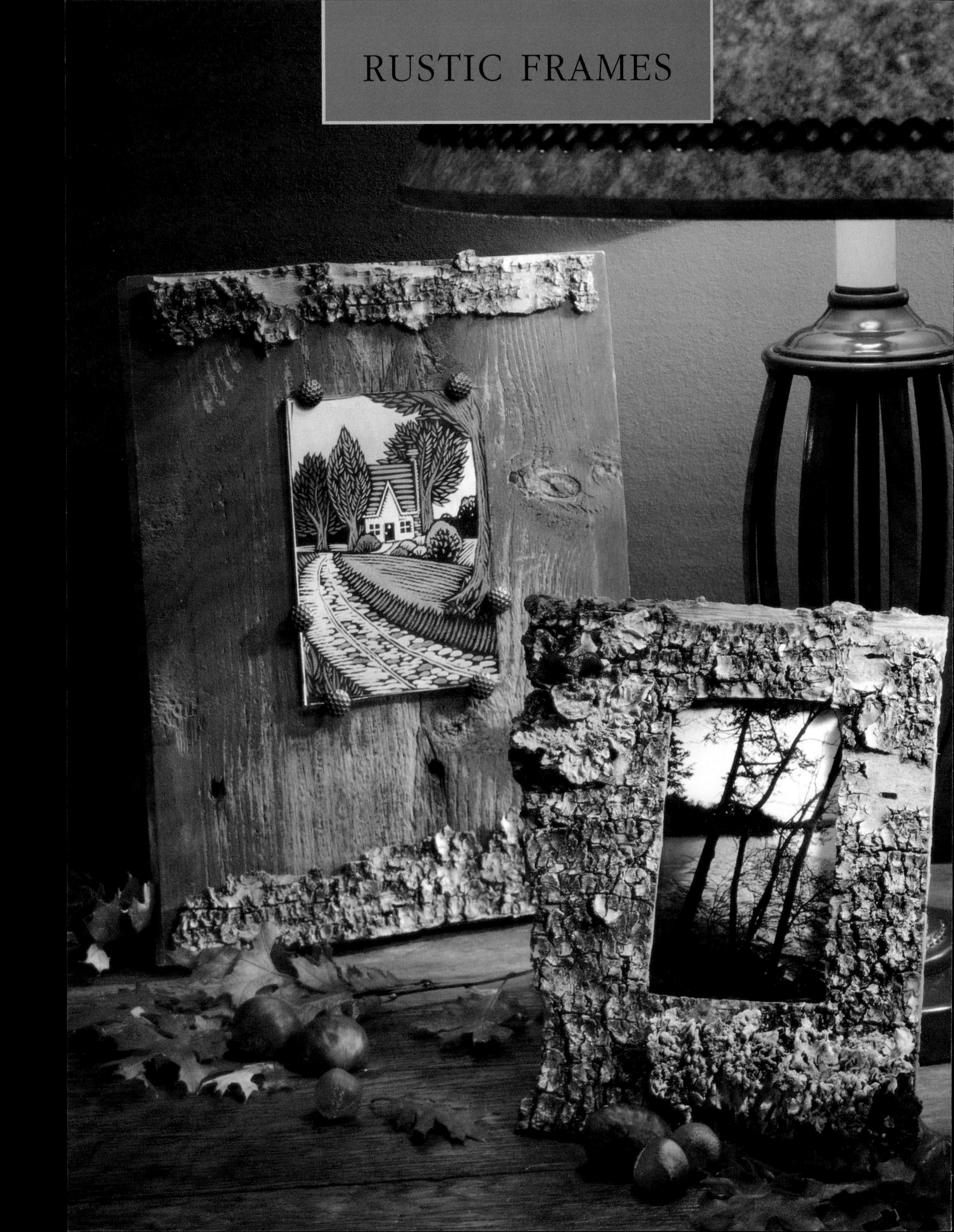

Simple rustic frames, created from weathered wood and tree bark, blend well in a country setting or add a surprising touch to a contemporary room. Collect loose tree bark from firewood or fallen trees. If the bark is not loose, cut it lengthwise with a utility knife and pry the bark away from the wood with a wood chisel or putty knife. Scrape off any excess fibrous material from the back of the bark. Flatten slightly curled bark by steaming it with an iron and pressing it between two boards until dry. Moisten severely curled bark, and seal it in a plastic bag until it is pliable enough to press flat.

HOW TO MAKE A BARK FRAME

MATERIALS

- Tree bark.
- Utility knife.
- Photograph or artwork.
- Glass and tools for cutting glass, as listed on page 100.
- Foam board, ⅜" (1 cm) thick.
- Hot glue gun and glue sticks.
- Mat board.
- Embellishments, such as lichens or moss, if desired.
- Self-adhesive hanger, if desired.

CUTTING DIRECTIONS

Cut the bark to the desired size, using a utility knife, or tear the bark to the desired size and shape. Cut the glass (page 100) to the same size as the photograph. Cut three spacers from foam board, ½" (1.3 cm) wide, with the length of one spacer equal to the length of the lower edge of the glass and the length of the remaining two spacers equal to the length of the sides of the glass. Cut a mat board backing 1" (2.5 cm) longer than the sides of the glass and 1¾" (4.5 cm) wider than the upper and lower edges of the glass. Cut a mat board shim the same size as the photograph.

1 Place the bark frame facedown on work surface. Mark opening in desired location on the back of the frame, with measurements ½" (1.3 cm) narrower and shorter than the width and length of the glass and photograph. Cut opening, using utility knife.

2 Glue foam board spacer for lower edge of opening to back of frame, using hot glue gun and centering spacer ¼" (6 mm) below opening. Glue the foam board spacers for the sides ⅜" (1 cm) beyond opening edges.

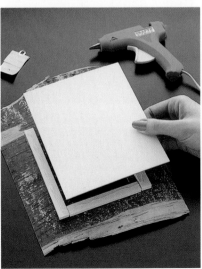

3 Glue the mat board backing over spacers; lower and side edges of the backing will extend ¼" (6 mm) beyond spacers. Attach a self-adhesive hanger, if desired.

4 Place the photograph facedown on glass; place mat board shim over the photograph; slide into place between the backing and the frame opening. Embellish with lichens or moss, if desired, gluing them to bark.

HOW TO MAKE A WEATHERED WOOD FRAME

MATERIALS

- Weathered wood.
- Artwork or photograph to be mounted.
- Glass and tools for cutting glass, as listed on page 100.
- Mat board for backing.
- Decorative upholstery tacks.
- Tack hammer.
- Two sawtooth hangers.
- Embellishments, such as lichens or moss, if desired.
- Hot glue gun and glue sticks.

CUTTING DIRECTIONS

Cut the weathered wood, if necessary, to the desired size. Cut the glass (page 100) and mat board backing to the same size as the artwork.

1 Attach sawtooth hanger to each top upper corner on back of frame.

2 Stack mat board backing, artwork, and glass in desired location on weathered wood frame.

3 Nail two decorative upholstery tacks, evenly spaced along each side of stack, with shanks of tacks close to, but not touching, glass and underside of tack heads just above glass.

4 Embellish with lichens or moss, if desired, using hot glue gun.

MORE IDEAS
FOR FRAMES

Copper mounting plate *with verdigris finish provides a backdrop for artwork encased in copper foil frame (page 98).*

Scuff copper sheet with sandpaper. Apply verdigris finish, following manufacturer's instructions. Mount copper foil frame, using hot glue.

Mark the desired opening. Drill holes in four corners of marked opening with large drill bit. Cut opening, using jigsaw; insert blade of jigsaw into drilled holes, and cut along marked lines.

Weathered wood frame *features rough cut openings for photographs. Back of frame is constructed like bark frame on page 103.*

RUB-ON TRANSFERS

To add instant design details to furniture, accessories, or ceramic tile, use rub-on transfers. Available in any decorating style from country to contemporary, rub-on transfers give the look of hand painting or stenciling in a fraction of the time. They can be purchased as single motifs or borders, in multicolored or monochromatic designs, as well as lettering and graphic motifs. Rub-on transfers that resemble etched glass are also available for use on glass and clear acrylic.

Follow the manufacturer's instructions for the application and cleaning of rub-on transfers. Generally, they are easily applied to any smooth, hard surface by placing the transfer facedown on the surface and rubbing over it, using a burnishing tool or craft stick. The transfers are not permanent, yet are durable enough to be washed gently; some brands are even dishwasher safe. When used on furniture and accessories, apply an aerosol clear acrylic sealer to the finished project for added durability.

HOW TO APPLY A RUB-ON TRANSFER

1 Remove the protective backing from transfer sheet. If several transfers are on one sheet, cut out the desired transfer. Place the transfer facedown on hard surface.

2 Hold transfer firmly in place; rub over transfer, using burnishing tool or craft stick.

3 Lift transfer sheet slowly, taking care that entire transfer is released from sheet. Cover the transfer with backing sheet; rub over transfer again, to secure it firmly.

SWITCH PLATE COVER-UPS

Ordinary plastic switch plates can be quickly transformed into attractive room accents, using a variety of craft materials. Smooth fabric or decorative paper can be applied, using decoupage medium. This results in a sealed surface that can be easily cleaned. Other materials, such as leather or tapestry fabrics, can be applied, using craft glue. For added dimension, mitered moldings or layers of tree bark can be attached to the switch plate.

Marbleized paper (a) *turns an ordinary switch plate into a contemporary accent.*

Switch plate embellished with tree bark and twigs (b) *adds a woodsy appeal.*

Fabric decoupage switch plate (c) *repeats a pattern used elsewhere in the room.*

Leather (d) *covers a switch plate for a masculine setting.*

Rich tapestry fabric (e) *on a switch plate complements the formal tone of a room. Narrow molding frames the outer edge.*

Seed packet (f) *applied to a switch plate becomes a whimsical country accent.*

HOW TO MAKE A DECOUPAGE SWITCH PLATE

MATERIALS

- Switch plate.
- Smooth, lightweight fabric or decorative paper.
- Mat knife or small, sharp scissors.
- Sponge applicator.

- Decoupage medium.
- Extra-fine sandpaper.
- Acrylic paint and small brush, to paint screw heads, if necessary.
- Awl.

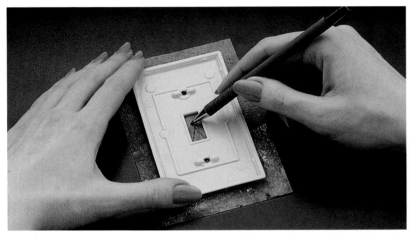

1 Cut fabric or paper 1" (2.5 cm) wider and longer than width and length of switch plate. Center switch plate facedown on wrong side of fabric or paper. Mark diagonal lines from corners in opening; cut on marked lines, using mat knife or small, sharp scissors.

2 Apply decoupage medium to wrong side of the fabric or paper, covering the entire area. Affix fabric or paper to front of switch plate, aligning diagonal cuts to opening.

HOW TO COVER A SWITCH PLATE WITH BARK

MATERIALS

- Switch plate.
- Tree bark.
- Mat knife.
- Thin, straight twigs.
- Hot glue gun and glue sticks.
- Awl.
- Acrylic paint and small brush, to paint screw heads, if necessary.

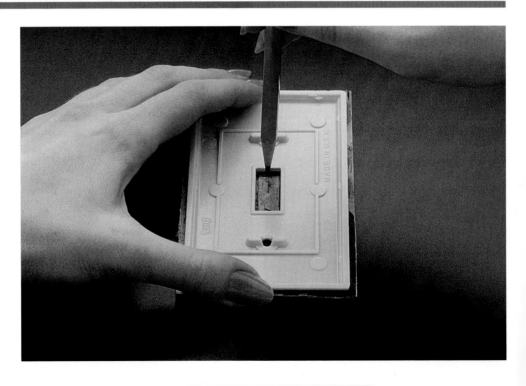

1 Cut bark ¼" (6 mm) wider and longer than the width and length of the switch plate, using mat knife. Center switch plate facedown on the wrong side of bark; trace and cut out the opening.

3 Smooth the fabric or paper in place, removing any bubbles. Wrap the outer edges around to back of the switch plate, folding out excess at corners. Wrap the points of fabric or paper to the back of switch plate at opening. Allow to dry.

4 Apply decoupage medium to the front and wrapped edges of the switch plate; allow to dry. Sand with extra-fine sandpaper, if necessary. Apply second coat of decoupage medium; allow to dry.

5 Paint screw heads, if necessary, using acrylic paint. Poke screw holes through fabric or paper, using awl; affix switch plate to wall.

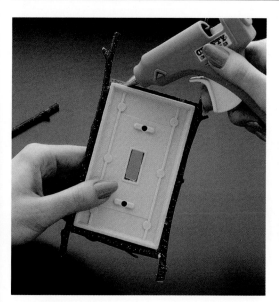

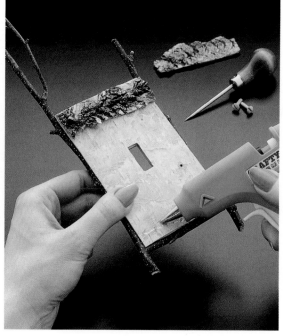

2 Glue bark to front of the switch plate, using hot glue gun. Glue thin, straight twigs along outer edges, just under the 1/8" (3 mm) extended edges of the bark.

3 Embellish with additional small pieces of tree bark, if desired. Paint the screw heads, if necessary, using acrylic paint. Punch screw holes through the bark, using awl; affix switch plate to the wall.

HOW TO COVER A SWITCH PLATE
WITH LEATHER OR TAPESTRY

MATERIALS

- Switch plate.
- Leather or tapestry.
- Mat knife or small, sharp scissors.
- Craft glue.
- Acrylic paint and small brush, to paint screw heads, if necessary.
- Awl.

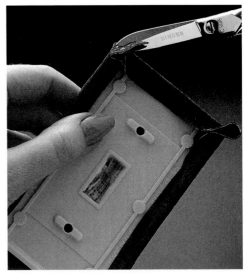

1 Cut leather or tapestry 1" (2.5 cm) wider and longer than width and length of switch plate. Apply craft glue to wrong side of leather or tapestry, covering entire area.

2 Affix leather or tapestry to front of switch plate. Smooth in place, removing any bubbles. Wrap outer edges of leather or tapestry around to back of switch plate. Trim out excess at corners to reduce bulk. Allow to dry.

HOW TO EMBELLISH A SWITCH PLATE
WITH DECORATIVE MOLDING

MATERIALS

- Switch plate.
- Material for inset, such as fabric, paper, or leather.
- Craft glue.
- Mat knife or small, sharp scissors.

- Narrow decorative molding.
- Miter box and backsaw.
- Wood glue.
- Masking tape.
- Spray paint.
- Awl.

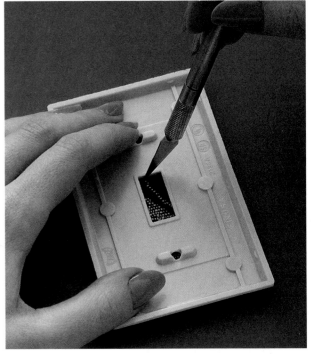

1 Cut inset ¾" (2 cm) narrower and shorter than width and length of switch plate. Apply craft glue to wrong side of inset; affix to center of switch plate. Allow to dry.

2 Cut material from the center opening, using mat knife or small scissors.

3 Cut the leather or tapestry from center opening, using mat knife or small scissors. Paint screw heads, if necessary, using acrylic paint. Punch screw holes through leather or fabric, using awl; affix switch plate to the wall.

3 Cut the molding pieces to form rectangle with mitered corners, using miter box and backsaw. Outer measurements of molding should be ¼" (6 mm) narrower and shorter than outer measurements of switch plate.

4 Glue the molding pieces together at corners, using wood glue. Glue molding to the switch plate, centering the rectangle over the inset.

5 Cover the inset with masking tape. Paint molding and outer edges of the switch plate. Paint screw heads, if necessary. Remove masking tape. Punch screw holes through the inset, using awl; affix the switch plate to the wall.

CUSTOMIZED LAMP SHADES

With minimal time and a little creativity, inexpensive lamp shades can be customized to fit any decorating plan. Lamp shades, constructed of either fabric or paper, are available in assorted sizes and shapes to suit a wide variety of lamp bases. The color of the shade can be changed by painting, either with spray paint or craft acrylic paint. Select a lamp shade that is slightly shorter than the height of the lamp base and covers the light socket when viewed from eye level.

Lamp shade embellishments should be suitable to the design of the base. Simple embellishments, such as lacing around the upper and lower edges of the shade, are appropriate for a very decorative or patterned lamp base. Metal nail heads on a lamp shade are a nice accent with a metal lamp base. Lamp shades with decoupage embellishments become the focal point when paired with plain ceramic lamp bases.

Colorful decoupage lamp shade (opposite) perks up a plain lamp base. Clip designs from wrapping paper or fabric, or use any flat material, such as pressed flowers or postage stamps, for embellishments.

Geometric nail heads (opposite) arranged along the lower edge of a lamp shade are a fitting complement to a traditional brass lamp base.

Decorative cord (left) is laced at the upper and lower edges of a fabric lamp shade, quietly repeating the dominant color in the patterned lamp base.

HOW TO MAKE A DECOUPAGE LAMP SHADE

MATERIALS

- Fabric or paper lamp shade.
- Thin, flat embellishments, such as paper or fabric cutouts, pressed flowers, postage stamps.
- Removable tape.
- Decoupage medium.
- Sponge applicator.

1 Arrange embellishments on shade surface, using removable tape. Apply decoupage medium to the wrong side of embellishment, using sponge applicator and covering entire area. Affix embellishment to outer surface of the shade in the desired position; smooth out any wrinkles or bubbles, using fingers. Repeat for any additional embellishments. Allow to dry.

2 Apply an even coat of decoupage medium to entire outer surface of shade. Allow to dry. Repeat, if desired.

HOW TO EMBELLISH A LAMP SHADE WITH METAL NAIL HEADS

MATERIALS

- Fabric or paper lamp shade.
- Metal nail heads in desired shapes and sizes.
- Pencil, for marking.
- Unsharpened wooden pencil with rubber eraser, for attaching nail heads.

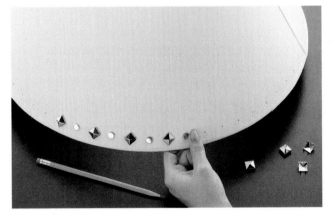

1 Plan placement of nail heads on the surface of shade; mark lightly with a pencil. Push prongs of the nail heads into the shade surface at marks.

2 Turn the shade facedown on work surface; work the prongs through to inside of the shade, using eraser end of pencil.

3 Press prongs down toward center of nail head, using blunt end of unsharpened pencil.

HOW TO APPLY LACING TO EDGES OF SHADE

MATERIALS

- Fabric or paper lamp shade.
- Lacing material, such as decorative cord, leather lacing, or twine, depending on the desired look.
- Hole punch set with changeable blades, wooden or rubber mallet, cutting mat, for punching holes.
- Craft glue.

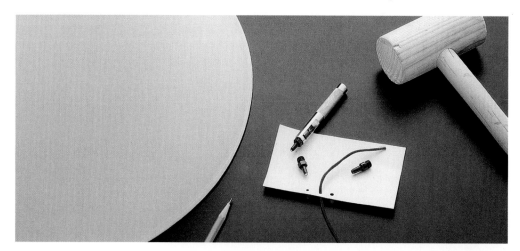

1 Determine correct size of hole for lacing material, by testing on scrap of heavy paper. Hole should be just large enough for easy insertion of the lacing material. Mark the placement for holes on inside of the shade, about 1½" (3.8 cm) apart and ⅜" (1 cm) from edge of the shade, beginning ¾" (2 cm) from the back seam. Adjust the marks, if necessary.

2 Lay shade facedown on the cutting mat. Align blade of hole punch tool to mark for hole; hold handle of tool perpendicular to shade surface. Strike end of handle with rubber or wooden mallet, cutting hole in shade. Repeat for all marked holes.

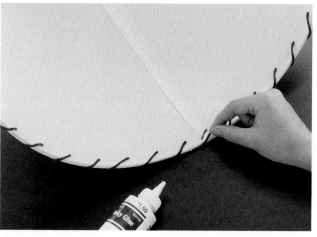

3 Insert lacing material through first hole at back seam; whipstitch around shade edge, leaving 3" (7.5 cm) tails at beginning and end.

4 Overlap the ends ½" (1.3 cm) on inside edge of the shade; trim excess. Glue in place, using craft glue.

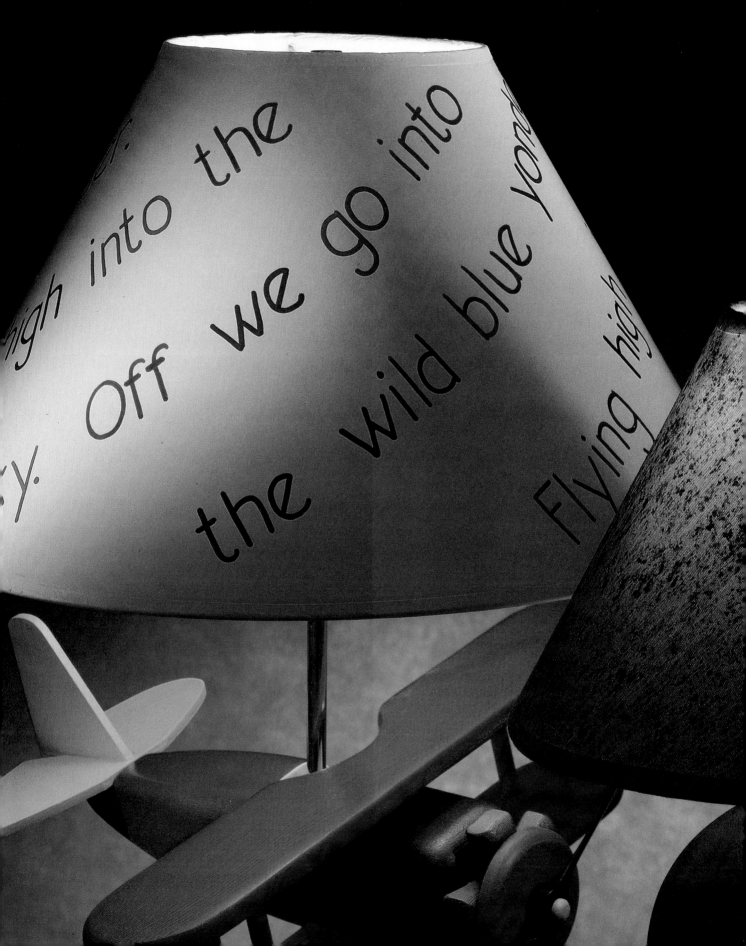

Leather lacing (right) in cross-stitch pattern adds a rustic accent to this lamp shade. Lower holes are spaced ½" (1.3 cm) apart; holes in upper row are positioned ½" (1.3 cm) directly above lower holes.

Stitch diagonally around entire shade, beginning at seam. Reverse direction, crossing first stitches in second pass.

Tassel fringe on the lower edge of the lamp shade (above) combines with the cut glass lamp base to make an elegant statement. Apply fringe to the lamp shade, using craft or fabric glue.

Sponge-painted lamp shade (left) has a textured look to contrast with the smooth ceramic lamp base. The shade was first spray painted a soft shade of lavender.

Paint pens were used to add a colorful touch of whimsy to the lamp shade on this child's lamp (opposite).

Apply speckles of paint, using a natural sea sponge.

Terra-cotta pots, whether new or aged, lend rustic appeal to decorative accessories. Cracked or broken pots are given new life when reduced to shards and used creatively. For a mosaic effect, small irregular shards are loosely pieced over a bed of sheet moss, transforming an ordinary item into a one-of-a-kind accessory. A terra-cotta wreath, constructed from fragmented pots and adorned with a bit of moss and raffia, is a unique wall accent.

HOW TO BREAK TERRA-COTTA POTS

MATERIALS

- Small terra-cotta pots, new or aged.
- Cardboard box; terry cloth towel; hammer.

1 Place several small terra-cotta pots in cardboard box; cover pots with terry cloth towel.

2 Strike pots through the towel with hammer. Lift towel; turn the large shards so outer curve faces upward. Replace towel; strike shards, breaking them into small pieces, 3/4" to 3" (2 to 7.5 cm) in size.

HOW TO MAKE A TERRA-COTTA MOSAIC ACCESSORY

MATERIALS

- Accessory to be covered, such as a vase, box, plant container, or bowl.
- Terra-cotta shards, ¾" to 2" (2 to 5 cm) in size.

- Hot glue gun and glue sticks.
- Fresh sheet moss.

1 Cover surface of accessory with sheet moss, securing moss with hot glue. Mist moss lightly, if desired, to make it more pliable.

2 Secure shards to accessory over moss, using hot glue gun; space shards about ¼" (6 mm) apart, allowing moss to show through.

HOW TO MAKE A TERRA-COTTA WREATH

MATERIALS

- Firm cardboard.
- Braided picture wire.
- Terra-cotta shards, 1" to 3" (2.5 to 7.5 cm) in size.

- Hot glue gun and glue sticks.
- Embellishments, such as moss, dried flowers, and raffia.

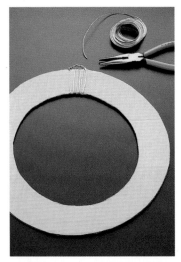

1 Cut wreath base from firm cardboard to the desired size and shape. Attach wire hanger to base as shown.

2 Glue a layer of terra-cotta shards to the wreath base, using hot glue gun. Glue additional layers of shards to wreath, staggering placement of shards and building layers to desired fullness.

3 Embellish with moss, dried flowers, and raffia bow.

MORE TERRA-COTTA ACCESSORIES

Terra-cotta mosaic balls *fill a decorative bowl, creating an interesting accent piece.*

Terra-cotta shards *adorn the outer edges of a rustic picture frame.*

SHELF EDGINGS

Shelf edgings are a quick way to add a personal touch to a room. Various materials can be used for shelf edgings, coordinating with any decorating style. Most materials can be easily applied to the shelf edges using double-stick ATG tape available at art supply and framing supply stores.

Ribbon *may be used alone as a shelf edging or as a backgound to which other materials, such as buttons, beads, shells, or nail heads, may be attached.*

Art paper, *fan-folded and cut to the desired shape, may be used to enhance a shelf edge in a contemporary room.*

Apply liquid fray preventer to ends of upholstery trims, laces, or ribbons to keep them from raveling.

Upholstery trims *are useful for shelf edgings in a traditional setting.*

Lace edgings *are a soft, feminine way to accent shelves.*

INDEX

A

Accents, floral,
  see: floral accents
Accessories, creative,
  copper foil picture frames, 98-101
  customized lamp shades, 115-119
  rub-on transfers, 107
  rustic frames, 102-105
  shelf edgings, 124-125
  spray painting, 92-97
  switch plate cover-ups, 108-113
  terra-cotta, 120-123
Armchairs, slipcovers for, 8-11
Arrangements, floral,
  see: floral arrangements

B

Bark frame, 103
Basket, moss-wrapped, for flowers, 74
Bed canopies, triangular, 26-30
Bed skirts, instant, 31
Birch-bark vase, 73
Bolster pillows, 32-33
Borders, creative wall, 52-57
Bottles, as vases, 75
Bow, cluster, 70-71

C

Canopies, triangular bed, 26-30
Chairs, slipcovers for, 8-17
Cluster bow, 70-71
Color washing walls, 46-47
Containers for fresh flowers, 72-75
Copper foil picture frames, 98-101
Covers, seat, from kitchen towels,
  14-15, 17
Cover-ups, switch plate, 108-113
Crackled finish, creating with spray
  paint, 97
Cutting glass for picture frames,
  100-101

D

Designs for walls, painted freehand,
  48-51
Displays, quick floral, 84-89
Draped window treatments, 20-25
Dried flowers, arrangements, 77, 80-82

E

Edgings, shelf, 124-125

F

Fabric, decorating with,
  linens, 14-19
  simple slipcovers, 8-13
Faux stone finish, creating with spray
  paint, 97
Finishes created with spray paint, 97
Flanged pillows, 35-37
Floral accents,
  arrangements, 77-83
  displays, 84-89
  easy grapevine wreaths, 67-71
  fresh flower containers, 72-75
Floral arrangements,
  dried, 77, 80-82
  quick displays, 84-89
  silk, 77, 80-81
  single-variety, 77-81
Flowers,
  arrangements, 77-83
  containers for, 72-75
Found objects, displays with, 84, 89
Frames,
  copper foil, 98-101
  rustic, 102-105
Freehand painted designs for walls,
  48-51
Fresh flowers, single-variety
  arrangements, 77-79
Fringed pillows, 35, 38
Furniture,
  decorating with linens, 14-19
  slipcovers for, 8-13

G

Glass, cutting for picture frames,
  100-101
Grapevine wreaths, 67-71

J

Jar, as vase, 75
Jelly roll bolster pillow, 32-33

K

Kitchen towels, as seat covers,
  14-15, 17
Knife-edge pillows, 39

L

Lamp shades, customized, 115-119
Linens, to decorate furniture, 14-19

M

Mantel cloth, from napkins, 19
Moss-wrapped flower basket, 74

N

Napkins,
  as a mantel cloth, 19
  as pillow slipcovers, 39

O

Ottoman, slipcover for, 18

P

Painted designs for walls, freehand,
  48-51
Picture frames,
  copper foil, 98-101
  rustic, 102-105
Pillowcases, as slipcovers, 14-17
Pillows,
  bolster, 32-33
  flanged, 35-37
  fringed, 35, 38
  quick, using napkins, 39
Plants, potted, display of, 86-87
Potted plants, display of, 86-87

Q

Quick floral displays, 84-89
Quick pillows, using napkins, 39

R

Ribbon-framed walls, 59-63
Rosette bolster pillow, 32-33
Rub-on transfers, 107
Rustic frames, 102-105

S

Seat covers, from kitchen towels,
  14-15, 17
Shades, customized lamp, 115-119
Shelf edgings, 124-125
Silhouette, creating with spray
  paint, 94, 96
Silk flowers, single-variety
  arrangements, 77, 80-81
Skirts, instant bed, 31
Slipcovers, simple, 8-18, 39
Sofa, slipcover for, 13
Spray painting,
  special effects, 94-97
  techniques, 92-93
Stenciling with spray paint, 94-95
Switch plate cover-ups, 108-113

T

Table runners, to decorate furniture,
  14, 19
Table topper, as an ottoman
  slipcover, 18
Terra-cotta accessories, 120-123
Texturizing techniques to decorate
  walls, 42-45
Towels, as seat covers, 14-15, 17
Transfers, rub-on, 107
Triangular bed canopies, 26-30

V

Vases,
  birch-bark, 73
  jars and bottles, 75

W

Wall borders, creative, 52-57
Walls, decorating,
  color washing, 47
  creative borders, 52-57
  freehand painted designs, 48-51
  ribbon-framed, 59-63
  texturizing techniques with paint,
    42-45
Weathered wood frame, 104-105
Window treatments, draped, 20-25
Wood frame, weathered, 104-105
Wreaths,
  display of, 84, 88
  grapevine, 67-71
  terra-cotta, 120-122

CREDITS

President/COO: Nino Tarantino
Executive V.P./Editor-in-Chief:
William B. Jones

HOME ACCENTS IN A FLASH
Created by: The Editors of
Cowles Creative Publishing, Inc.

Books available in this series:
Bedroom Decorating, Creative Window Treatments, Decorating for Christmas, Decorating the Living Room, Creative Accessories for the Home, Decorating with Silk & Dried Flowers, Kitchen & Bathroom Ideas, Decorating the Kitchen, Decorative Painting, Decorating Your Home for Christmas, Decorating for Dining & Entertaining, Decorating with Fabric & Wallcovering, Decorating the Bathroom, Decorating with Great Finds, Affordable Decorating, Picture-Perfect Walls, More Creative Window Treatments, Outdoor Decor, The Gift of Christmas, Home Accents in a Flash, Painted Illusions

Group Executive Editor: Zoe A. Graul
Editorial Manager: Dawn M. Anderson
Project Manager: Elaine Johnson
Associate Creative Director:
Lisa Rosenthal

Art Director: Stephanie Michaud
Writer: Linda Neubauer
Editor: Janice Cauley
Researcher/Designer: Michael Basler
Researcher: Linda Neubauer
Sample Production Manager:
Carol Olson
Senior Technical Photo Stylist:
Bridget Haugh
Technical Photo Stylists: Sue Jorgensen,
Nancy Sundeen
Styling Director: Bobbette Destiche
Project Stylist: Coralie Sathre
Prop Stylist: Michele Joy
Lead Artisan: Phyllis Galbraith
Artisans: Arlene Dohrman,
Phyllis Galbraith, Carol Pilot,
Michelle Skudlarek, Nancy Sundeen
*Vice President of Development Planning
& Production:* Jim Bindas
Director of Photography: Mike Parker
Studio Manager: Marcia Chambers
Lead Photographer: Charles Nields
Lead Assistant: Greg Wallace
Photographers: Rex Irmen, Bill Lindner,
Mark Macemon, Rebecca Schmitt
Contributing Photographer: Steve Smith
Print Production Manager: Patt Sizer
Senior Desktop Publishing Specialist:
Joe Fahey
Desktop Publishing Specialist:
Laurie Kristensen
Production Staff: Laura Hokkanen, Tom
Hoops, Jeanette Moss, Mike Schauer,
Mike Sipe, Brent Thomas, Kay Wethern
Shop Supervisor: Phil Juntti
Scenic Carpenters: Troy Johnson,

Rob Johnstone, John Nadeau
Contributors: Carnival/Color Bolt;
Conso Products Company; Design
Master; Graber Industries, Inc./Springs
Window Fashion Division; Kirsch
Division, Cooper Industries, Inc.;
Minnetonka Mills, Inc.; Offray Ribbon;
Plaid Enterprises; Putnam Company,
Inc.; Tolin' Station; Waverly, Division
of F. Schumacher & Company;
Wayzata Lamps & Shades; Windmill
Imports, Inc.
Sources for Product Information:
Copper Verdigris Solution/Patina
Green, p. 105—MODERN OPTIONS,
2325 3rd Street, #339, San Francisco,
CA 94107, (415) 252-5580;
Crackle Spray Paint, p. 97—Carnival/
Color Bolt, P.O. Box 4656, Scottsdale,
AZ 85261, 1-800-527-4799;
Lamps and Shades, pp. 114-119—
Wayzata Lamps & Shades, 1250 E.
Wayzata Blvd., Wayzata, MN 55391,
(612) 449-9802
Printed on American paper by:
Quebecor Printing
00 99 98 97 / 5 4 3 2 1

Cowles Creative Publishing, Inc. offers
a variety of how-to books. For
information write:
Cowles Creative Publishing
Subscriber Books
5900 Green Oak Drive
Minnetonka, MN 55343